IN THE MEANTIME....

Learning to Live in Difficult Times

Ronald Higdon

IN THE MEANTIME

Learning to Live In Difficult Times

Ronald Higdon

Parson's Porch Books

ISBN: Softcover 978-1-936912-45-2

This book was printed in the United States of America.

To order additional copies of this book, contact:

Parson's Porch Books
1-423-475-7308
www.parsonsporch.com

Acknowledgments

This book contains many reflections from my experiences with various congregations with whom I have worked over the past fifty-plus years. As the years have increased so has my appreciation for the significant contribution all of these congregations have made to my life and my ministry. I list all of them with gratitude and appreciation – perhaps especially for the difficult times that I often found a way to make more difficult. These times usually provided the opportunities for the most learning. Why is it we only recognize this after the fact? Well, such is life, but may it always be as Paul admonishes: *in everything…with thanksgiving* (Phil. 4:6). It is with thanksgiving that I dedicate this book to the following congregations:

(Student Ministry):

Old Cedar Baptist Church; Owen County, Kentucky
Vine Run Baptist Church; Grant County, Kentucky

(Pastorates):

Pine Street Baptist Church; Richmond, Virginia
First Baptist Church; Rocky Mount, North Carolina
First Baptist Church; Waynesboro, Virginia
Broadway Baptist Church; Louisville, Kentucky

(Interim Pastorates):

Latonia Baptist Church, Covington, Kentucky
First Baptist Church; Corbin, Kentucky
First Baptist Church; Williamsburg, Kentucky
Highland Park Baptist Church; Austin, Texas
First Baptist Church; Athens, Georgia
Speedway Baptist Church; Speedway, Indiana

Table of Contents

Introduction

An unexamined faith is not worth living," a twist on Socrates' famous dictum, "An unexamined life is not worth living," is the essential challenge for those of us who find ourselves living in the challenging and most rapidly changing times the world has ever known. The temptation is to run for cover. To retreat. To weep for what was and will never be again. To hunker down in some sort of protective shell. What we really need is a faith that is deep enough, biblical enough, and hopeful enough to enable us to be fully alive and fully invested in the only time we have - right now. That is the purpose of this book, *In the Meantime: Learning to Live in Difficult Times.*

I never want to promise too much because that would make it appear I speak as an authority, as one who has achieved what he is offering to others. How I wish I had lived fully and powerfully in all those times I was waiting for better circumstances and opportunities to arrive. But I do think I have learned some lessons along the way and it is these lessons, based on some striking and often startling texts, that I want to pass along.

This book is peppered with personal stories, not so much about achievements and victories, but with an unspoken "I could have responded in that situation differently and more redemptively for everyone concerned." These reminiscences (given only as I remember them) are meant to remind me of lessons that can now be applied to the present with gratitude that I have learned some things along the way. Because I believe in the Old Boy's Law, "You never learn anything the second time you're kicked by a mule," I have attempted to make new mistakes – and usually have succeeded! Hopefully, these stories will aid you in processing some of your own stories and enable you to join me in making new mistakes.

However, this book does not major on mistakes but on the specific ways in which we can say with conviction: *This is the day the Lord has made; let us rejoice and be glad in it* (Psalm 118:24). Many find this exceedingly difficult in the context of our time. We continue to struggle with the most severe economic downturn since the Great Depression, the new global dimensions of our world that have brought both frustration and fear, visible world unrest that enters our lives through daily news reporting, armed conflict that shows no sign of abating, instant and proliferating methods of communication that have produced a cacophony of conflicting "facts" and points of view, scandals that continue to rock the foundations of our economic system, our political system, and our sports' world (currently focused on Penn State). To all this is added "a rare astronomical event: the alignment of the Earth and the Sun with the 'dark rift' at the center of the Milky Way on the winter solstice of December 21, 2012...an event that occurs once every 25,800 years."[1] As the Mayan calendar ends, some contend so will everything else.

My thesis is that we can make progress in learning to live fully and powerfully with all this – with what is. Question: How can we live with what is not? Question: Can we really postpone living until better times arrive? Question: When does life "happen"? Sue Monk Kidd speaks for entirely too many: "Mostly I saw life 'happening' in the future. It can be jolting to discover how much of life we project there....We think the 'real thing' is concentrated in the *next* moment, the *next* month, the next year..."[2]

Jean-Pierre de Caussade wrote in *Abandonment to Divine Providence* that the single most important concern of the soul is to seek and accept the present moment. "The present moment is always overflowing with immeasurable riches, far more than you are able to hold."[3] Whether you see this as a gross exaggeration or an unreachable goal, it is the basic challenge faced by most of us most of the time because most of life is filled with "in the meantime" circumstances. We're just waiting to get through something. But while we are waiting life is happening. The old cliché is true: no part of life is a dress rehearsal.

This book is divided into four parts with three chapters in each division. Each chapter is followed by "Points to Ponder" and each division is followed by "Reflections." My purpose is to encourage self-reflection and conversation. Part I illustrates two approaches to meantime situations: exiles in Babylon find it impossible to sing the Lord's song; Paul and Silas are able to belt out hymns at midnight in a prison cell. Part II calls for the challenges of bringing mountaintop perspectives to valley living - what I like to call "high tone living during low tone times." Part III lists some priorities that literally can be life and situation changing. Part IV suggests unique opportunities that are particularly available in the "meantimes." The conclusion is the reminder that biblical faith is always a tough faith for tough times.

It bears repeating that the bibliography of quoted sources reveals a diverse array of voices coming from varying perspectives. Some controversial authors and books have been used. My personal reading has never been restricted to what I often refer to as "safe" reads. Meaning: they only confirm what I already believe, don't really challenge my ideas, and can be in plain sight for public inspection - even by heresy hunters. I have discovered some of the best questions ever asked and some of the best ideas ever offered in the writings of some considered to be the most unorthodox. The citing of a book does not imply that I endorse everything the author says. I often quip in Bible studies that I don't endorse everything I've said! Why are we so fearful of having our beliefs challenged? This doesn't mean we abandon everything we believe but if I cannot bear to have anything I believe questioned, I question how strong and solid my beliefs actually are.

I once quoted Leslie Weatherhead when preaching as a guest at a church in England and a considerable number of those present in the congregation that day did not return for subsequent sermons. Such a liberal was not to be heard on any subject! I don't know if they were aware that one of the best books ever written on the will of God (and endorsed by almost everyone) is Weatherhead's 56 page book, *The Will of God.*[4] Many have found comfort and consolation in the five chapters: God's Intentional Will; God's Circumstantial Will; God's Ultimate Will; Discerning the Will of God; "In His Will Is Our Peace."

I ask that you not slam shut this book if you find an outrageous quote from an outrageous writer. After all, there are some pretty outrageous things in the Bible! (Another book in the hopper is "Things You Might Be Surprised to Find in the Bible." I once did a two-session Bible study in which we noted about seventy-five such texts.) Who knows? Such outrageous texts and outrageous quotes may be the very things that open our eyes to what we haven't seen before and open our ears to what we've never heard before.

My prayer is voiced in the request from another writer: "So receive the things I say not as formulas to live by but as hints, nudges, and clues that might help you on your way."[5]

Unless otherwise noted, Scripture references are from the New Revised Standard Version.

[1]Daniel Pinchbeck, *2012* (New York, Penguin Group, 2008), 12, 238.

[2]Sue Monk Kidd, *When the Heart Waits* (New York, HarperOne, 1990), 36-37.

[3]Ibid, 193-194.

[4]Leslie Weatherhead, *The Will of God* (Nashville, Abingdon Press, 1944).

[5]Spencer Burke, *Heretic's Guide to Eternity* (San Francisco, Jossey-Bass, 2006), 225.

Part I: What Time Is it?

Chapter 1: How Could We Sing the Lord's Song in a Foreign Land?

MODERN OBSERVATIONS:

Once a poor creature, now a wonder,
A wonder tortur'd in the space
Betwixt this world and that of grace.[1]

The relevance of Christianity to most Americans – then and now – has far more to do with the promise of eternal salvation *from* this world than with any desire to practice the teachings of Jesus while we are here.[2]

Ralph Waldo Emerson: "One of the illusions of life is that the present hour is not the critical decisive hour. Write it on your heart that every day is the best day of the year."[3]

Our crisis is the crisis of the disillusioned who have no frame of reference for the experience of disillusionment.[4]

When my mother died, having "made do" all her life, I found even her wedding gifts, unused, stashed away, "for a rainy day."[5]

"By and large Western civilization is a celebration of the illusion that good may exist without evil, light without darkness, and pleasure without pain, and this is true of both its Christian and secular technological phases....The history of spirituality tells us that we must learn to accept paradoxes, or we will never love anything or see it correctly." Alan Watts.[6]

THE BIBLICAL TEXTS: Psalm 137:1-4; Acts 16:23-25:

By the rivers of Babylon – there we sat down and there we wept when we remembered Zion. On the willows there we hung up our harps. For there our captors asked us for songs, and our tormentors asked for mirth, saying, "Sing us one of the songs of Zion!" How could we sing the Lord's song in a foreign land?

After they had given them a severe beating, they threw them into prison and ordered the jailer to keep them securely. Following these instructions, he put them in the innermost cell and fastened their feet in the stocks. About midnight Paul and Silas were praying and singing hymns to God, and the prisoners were listening to them.

A Study in Contrasts

The texts from Psalm 137 and Acts 16 provide the ultimate study in contrasts. Two extreme situations give rise to two totally different responses. One response I can easily understand; the second gives me reason to pause because, even on my best days, I cannot imagine it to be the kind of response I would make. And, of course, the purpose of these texts is not to berate the exiles for their lack of faith in God or to write off the bizarre behavior of Paul and Silas as the result of a martyr complex. As with all the biblical stories, we are to make them our stories.

The context of each situation seems clear enough. Psalm 137 finds the exiles in Babylon after both the Temple and Jerusalem lie in ruins. The unthinkable has happened. The prophets of doom and gloom were right after all. This psalm expresses the despair of a captive, deported people. Most commentators agree that "the psalm seems to be the voice of exiles who have returned to live in the ruins of a Jerusalem not yet rebuilt. The memories of their humiliation by and in Babylon are fresh...."[7]

The lament is especially poignant if it is read as the response to a taunt from their captors addressed to Temple musicians requesting one of "the songs of Zion." The request is an indirect attack on the God who appears to have met his match in a contest with the gods of Babylon. Asking for one of the hymns of praise that had been sung in the Temple at Jerusalem is almost in the category of excessive cruelty.

> The request was intended as an insult to the exiles' God, similar to the derogatory question, "Where is your God?" Captors and captives alike were very clear that the issue was not music; it was faith. There could be no hymns of joy in Babylon. That would have been betrayal, singing joyous songs of the sovereignty of the Lord in a territory that represented another sovereignty.[8]

In Acts 16, we find Paul and Silas imprisoned in Philippi (a Roman colony) for disrupting the local economy by exorcising the demons from a slave girl and "*throwing our city into an uproar by advocating customs unlawful for us Romans to accept or practice*" (20-21; *New International Version*). After being severely flogged, they are placed in the innermost cell with their feet fastened in stocks. "One would expect that after such brutal treatment, Paul and Silas would be bemoaning their plight. Certainly they were suffering pain and shock from the flogging they had received."[9] My selection for a proper song in the midnight darkness would have been: *Nobody knows the trouble I've seen.* It is to be noted that the jailer has to have torches to light his way to the cell (16:29). He's checking out the strange sounds coming from within the darkness: Paul and Silas are belting out *a robust hymn to God. The other prisoners couldn't believe their ears* (16:25; *The Message).*

When the Unthinkable Happens

The national assumption and the theme of orthodox teaching was that the Temple was inviolate and Jerusalem was always a safe haven beyond the reach of invaders. God's protection was certain; this is what he had promised to David and his descendants. The few negative voices of impending doom were written off as heretical ravings. Everyone knew what could never happen. The Northern Kingdom had fallen in 722 B.C.E. due to its unfaithfulness but they were never heir to promises concerning their capital (Samaria) as were those who were secure in Jerusalem with their Mount Zion. Destruction was unthinkable.

Paul was not unfamiliar with negative receptions and attempts on his life, but this appears to have been his first jail experience. Perhaps for Paul it was not all that unthinkable but for most of us this does not appear to be the "victorious Christian life" we have been promised. We view mob violence, stoning, beating, and imprisonment as something totally alien to our expectations. Hence, my protestation, "We won't be singing the Lord's songs until things get better. We have no songs for this kind of an interim - and we hope it is just that!"

Perhaps "unthinkable" is too strong a word for most of the things that come crashing into our lives as uninvited guests. Uninvited guests we need to get rid of as soon as possible so that things can get back to "normal" and we can begin to live again. This easily becomes a time for hunkering down and constantly lamenting our lot. Both the exiles in Babylon and Paul and Silas in jail were not imagining that things were worse than they were. No amount of positive thinking was going to bring about a change in the situations. After some "Oh, no!" moments, it was time to decide how life would be lived in the light of present realities.

Scott Peck's *The Road Less Traveled* was on the *New York Times* best-seller list for more than ten years and has sold millions of copies. It may surprise those who have never read it that the first three words in Chapter 1 are: "Life is difficult." "This is the simple observable truth that thrust M. Scott Peck onto the world stage."[10] A brief portion of Peck's first chapter is worth noting here:

> Life is difficult.
>
> This is a great truth, one of the greatest truths....Most do not fully see this truth that life is difficult. Instead they moan more or less incessantly, noisily or subtly, about the enormity of their problems, their burdens, and their difficulties as if life were generally easy, as if life *should* be easy.[11]

Somewhere along the way into the pastorate, I picked up the idea that when I found the "right" church, things would get a whole lot better. When I found that church I was certain my ministry would flourish and I would be treated as any successful pastor should be treated. And the critics would no longer occupy the front pews! (I continue to struggle with the profound truth that it is from our critics that we can sometimes learn the most. Note the "sometimes," which lets you know it continues to be a struggle!) Alas, I kept looking and hoping. Along the way, my younger son presented me with a Christmas gift that came with an explanation. As he presented *Fox's Book of Martyrs* to me, he said, "I bought this but was disappointed because I knew I would find your name in it." I confess that my complaining and lamenting were too much a part of my life. How I had missed the four most important words in seminary education I do not know: "The pastorate is difficult!"

But what isn't difficult?! It's not just the pastorate. Peck is correct. Life is difficult. Why is it so unthinkable that we have found it so? Why do we find it much easier to identify with the lamenting exiles in Babylon than with Paul and Silas? What are we supposed to do with life as it is? Is there any word from the Lord for this kind of a situation? There is and it sounds just as strange to us today as it did when it was uttered centuries ago.

The Biblical Prescription for Difficult Times (Jeremiah 29:4-7)

> *Thus says the Lord of hosts, the God of Israel to all the exiles whom I have sent into exile from Jerusalem to Babylon: Build houses and live in them, plant gardens and eat what they produce. Take wives and have sons and daughters; multiply there, and do not decrease. But seek the welfare of the city where I have sent you into exile and pray to the Lord on its behalf, for in its welfare you will find your welfare.*

My paraphrase of God's prescription for the exiles:

"Invest yourselves fully in life where you are and as it is right now. Don't hold back. Give it all you've got. You've spent enough time lamenting, now get rid of your self-pity and resentment. Be a model citizen in this foreign land and make it a better place for your being there."

Like most of God's prescriptions for living, this sounds like a prescription for saints (but, of course, that is the biblical term for all of us who call ourselves disciples). This prescription sounds very much like Matthew's Sermon on the Mount (chapters five through seven). In it, Jesus tells his followers how to live in a time of Roman occupation, heavy taxation, and unfulfilled messianic expectations. It is the clarion call for how to live in the interim between the Kingdom's inauguration in Jesus' ministry and the final consummation (completion) at the end of the age.

It is the way we live with the weeds that simply cannot be rooted out without destroying the wheat as well (Mark 4:1-9). As with most parables, this eyebrow raising story reminds us that we will never be able to eliminate all the weedy things in life. That doesn't mean that some weeds should not be rooted out; some are alarmingly destructive and Evil with a capital E. The continuing conundrum is figuring out how to eliminate them without inflicting greater damage. Another ever present temptation is to so focus on the weeds (the bad stuff) that one pays scant attention to the wheat (the good stuff). The world is as it has always been - an imperfect place where an immense number of things always need straightening out. To Illustrate: a couple of quotes:

> There isn't much middle ground in the debate on sex. You seldom hear an affirmation of hard-won sexual freedoms that is coupled with equally clear calls for my sexual responsibility – the only choices seem to be "no," or "anything goes."

> Even the Puritans knew that sexuality was hard to control in America....In the 1780s and 1790s, one-third of the brides in rural New England were pregnant at the time of marriage.[12]

I am not calling for the abandonment of moral and civic responsibility or for the toleration of injustice. Later we will discuss some perspectives and behaviors to keep in mind as we seek to live out our light and saltiness (Matthew 5:13-16) in a way that is a big cut above the way the Pharisees in Jesus' day saw their role. Jesus' forgotten warning, *Unless your righteousness exceeds that of the scribes and Pharisees, you will never enter the kingdom of heaven* (Matthew 5:20), is often too quickly dismissed with, "Well, I'm no hypocrite!" The warning has more ramifications than that. The Pharisees were among the best people of their day; they were defenders and keepers of the law. What they seemed to have lacked was the compassion and understanding that could keep them in touch with the masses of common people who needed mercy and not condemnation and rejection. (More about this in Chapter 9.)

"I have learned to cooperate with the inevitable" is the confession that some things are simply givens. A survey from a decade ago (that is probably still up to date) asked the question: "If you could change one thing about yourself, what would you change?" Nearly 90 percent of those surveyed pointed to things that they could not possibly alter.[13] The exiles were in Babylon, Paul and Silas were in a prison cell - facts. The question for all of us: In my present situation with what I cannot possibly change, how am I going to live positively and creatively - without becoming president of the "Poor Me Club"? Every day I need to ask: How can I invest myself fully in this present moment? Living by "if only" is not living! Take it from one who knows it by experience!

Is It Once Again the Control Issue?

Questions from those outside of the faith often provide excellent discussion topics for those of us inside the faith:

> My friend Mark from New York asked me more than once, "Why do you Christians want Christianity to win all the time? You don't seem to know how to live in a world where you aren't in charge."[14]

I'm probably stepping in over my head (my usual pulpit stance) when I contend that this may be the most important question for us to ask ourselves in this foreign postmodern world. The declining influence of the church in our culture (even in the South!) has taken many by surprise. It is too quickly assumed that the posting of the Ten Commandments will quickly resurrect our Judea-Christian heritage - however that is to be interpreted. We simply do not know how to live with the plurality of faiths and diverse expressions of "spirituality" that blend traditions from both the East and West. The famous line uttered by Dorothy in *The Wizard of Oz* just about sums up everything in our world: "I don't believe we're in Kansas anymore." The world in which most of us grew up is no more. I have lived to see the progression from 78 rpm records, to 33 1/3 long-play, 45 rpm, cassette and 8-tracks tapes, to cds, to nothing that can be examined in a "record store." Most young people today have no idea what a record store was! Most of my world is now available only in antique malls. And it's not coming back!

The above analogy might seem to imply that we are now living in the land of Oz (an imaginary land that Frank Baum invented by glancing at his filing cabinet and seeing one section labeled O – Z). Our world is more like the one Alice falls into when she tumbles down a rabbit hole where she encounters the Mad Hatter, Tweedledum and Tweedledee, a Cheshire Cat, the strange assortment at a Mad Tea Party, and the Queen of Hearts whose favorite phrase seems to be "Off with her head!" It is indeed "Wonderland" where one wonders what happened to order, predictability, and sense rather than nonsense.

I still believe that biblical faith can enable us to make some sense out of the nonsense that makes up far too much of our world. In our "What could possibly happen next?" world. The great saints we celebrate never abandoned their world while waiting for the next one to arrive. They lived remarkable lives in times marked by great challenges. May we so live as to find ourselves numbered among them.

[1]Rodney Clapp, *Tortured Wonders* (Grand Rapids, Brazos Press, 2006), 5.

[2]Eric Reece, *An American Gospel* (New York, Riverside Books, 2009), 71.

[3]Jan Karon, *A Continual Feast* (New York, Penguin Group, 2005), 118.

[4]Douglas John Hall, *Thinking the Faith* (Minneapolis, Augsburg, 1989), 197.

[5]W. Paul Jones, *Trumpet at Full Moon* (Louisville, Westminster/John Knox, 1992), 144.

[6]Richard Rohr, *The Naked Now* (New York, Crossroad Publishing, 2009), 143, 144.

[7]James L. Mays, *Interpretation: Psalms* (Louisville, John Knox, 1994), 421.

[8]Ibid, 422.

[9]*Expositor's Bible Commentary* (Grand Rapids, Zondervan, 1981), IX, 464.

[10]Matthew Kelly, *Perfectly Yourself* (New York, Ballantine Books, 2006), 202.

[11]Scott Peck, *The Road Less Traveled* (New York, Simon and Schuster, 1978), 15.

[12]David Callahan, *The Moral Center* (Orlando, Harcourt Books, 2006), 57, 59, 60.

[13]Terry Felber, *Am I Making Myself Clear?* (Nashville, Thomas Nelson, 2002), 36.

[14]Doug Pagitt and Tony Jones, *Emergent Manifesto of Hope* (Grand Rapids, Baker Books, 2007), 198.

How Could We Sing the Lord's Song in a Strange Land? Points To Ponder

The history of spirituality tells us that we must learn to accept paradoxes or we will never love anything or see it correctly.

As with all the biblical stories, we are to make them our stories.

(In Babylon) captors and captives alike were very clear that the issue was not music, it was faith.

Both the exiles in Babylon and Paul and Silas in jail were not imagining that things were worse than they were. No amount of positive thinking was going to bring about a change in the situation.

It may surprise those who have never read it, that the first three words in Chapter 1 (Scott Peck's *The Road Less Traveled)* are: "Life is difficult."

Why do we find it so much easier to identify with the lamenting exiles in Babylon than with Paul and Silas?

Another ever present temptation is to so focus on the weeds (the bad stuff) that one pays scant attention to the wheat (the good stuff).

The question for all of us: In my present situation with what I cannot possibly change, how am I going to live positively and creatively – without becoming president of the "Poor Me Club"?

Our world is more like the one Alice falls into when she tumbles down a rabbit hole.

Chapter 2: Searching for a Metaphor for Life

MODERN OBVERSATIONS:

I recently reread *The Pilgrim's Progress* and was struck anew by its psychological acuity....As our pilgrim soldiers on, he meets a full range of humanity: Mr. Talkative, Mr. Smooth-man, Mr. Facing-bothways, Mr. Anything (in our own day he would be Mr. Whatever), Mr. Money-love, Lord Time-server, and a parson, Mr. Two-tongues. Christian walks with Hopeful, the companion he had adopted by the banks of a river.[1]

We have inherited a set of metaphors all suggesting that energy is somehow stable and unchanging, but what characterizes energy more than anything else is a sense of movement and unfolding.[2]

There are two visions of life, two kinds of people. The first see life as a possession to be carefully guarded. They are called *settlers.* The second see life as a wild, fantastic, explosive gift. They are called *pioneers.* These two types give rise to two kinds of theology: Settler Theology and Pioneer Theology. Settler Theology is an attempt to answer all the questions, define and housebreak some sort of Supreme Being, establish the status quo on golden tablets in cinemascope. Pioneer Theology is an attempt to talk about what it means to receive the strange gift of life. The Wild West is the setting for both theologies.[3]

THE BIBLICAL TEXT: Hebrews 11:13-16:

All of these died in faith without having received the promises, but from a distance they saw and greeted them. They confessed that they were strangers and foreigners on the earth, for people who speak in this way make it clear that they are seeking a homeland. If they had been thinking of the land that they had left behind, they would have had no opportunity to return. But as it is, they desire a better country, that is, a heavenly one. Therefore God is not ashamed to be called their God; indeed, he has prepared a city for them.

In Search of a Metaphor

Perhaps the most famous metaphor for life has been given by Shakespeare:

> All the world's a stage,
> And all the men and women merely players...[4]

> Life's but a walking shadow, a poor player
> That struts and frets his hour upon the stage,
> And then is heard no more; it is a tale
> Told by an idiot, full of sound and fury,
> Signifying nothing.[5]

If you examine the full context of each of these quotations, you are immediately struck by the pessimism and cynicism inherent in them. Although *As You Like It* is called one of the happiest of Shakespeare's comedies (its classification should be noted), the idea of seven stages of life with the final stage culminating in *second childishness and mere oblivion, Sans teeth, sans eyes, sans taste, sans everything,* pictures life as pretty much as a downhill slide. Things only get worse as you get older. The end is marked by the word "*without*" (*sans).* The end is the absence of everything that made life worthwhile.

The Tragedy of Macbeth by its very title lets you know what you are in for. The above quotation from Macbeth gets even darker when we read his words immediately preceding it:

> Tomorrow, and tomorrow, and tomorrow,
> Creeps in this petty pace from day to day
> To the last syllable of recorded time;
> And all our yesterdays have lighted fools
> The way to dusty death. Out, out, brief candle!

The brevity and the futility of life take center stage in these speeches. There are many problems with the metaphor of the world as a stage and life as being a player on that stage. Finally the play ends and the curtain comes down; it's over. Then there is another play with another set of actors and actresses, but finally their run is over. "Playing a part" can certainly have a more positive application, but if our quoted actors played out their parts, they were certainly given tragic roles indeed. If they simply found their predetermined scripts and mouthed their predetermined lines, the world is more like the stage on which we are all merely puppets with the strings being pulled by one who views life as a cosmic joke.

A far more hopeful metaphor is one that can be found in almost every culture: the metaphor of life as a journey. It is the one given throughout Scripture but especially in Hebrews 11:13: *They confessed that they were strangers and foreigners on the earth.* I believe the better translation of the Greek word translated *foreigners* is *sojourners* or *pilgrims.* Life as pilgrimage is THE biblical metaphor for life. The author of Hebrews tells us that Abraham, Isaac, and Jacob lived in tents; they were nomads. They were constantly on the move. They looked for a city that had foundations, not tent pegs. They looked for something solid and permanent. They were pilgrims on a journey and hope was not only to be found at the end of the journey but everywhere along the way during that journey.

The Journeying is All Important

For such a serious subject, a double-dose of Charles Schultz' *Peanuts* seems to be in order:

Charlie Brown and Linus are standing behind the

> wall looking out. Charlie Brown has the speaking lines in all four scenes: "I never seem to know what's going on....Right from the very start my life has been strange....I think I know what happened....I must have missed all the rehearsals."
>
> In another conversation with Linus, Charlie Brown confesses: "Life is too much for me....I've been confused right from the day I was born....I think the whole trouble is that we're thrown into life too fast....We're not really prepared." Linus responds: "What did you want...a chance to warm up first?"

We don't get any warm ups or time outs. There is no saying, "This one doesn't count! This is just for practice!" Everything counts. Everything is a part of the pilgrimage. Rather than this concept diminishing life, it intensifies the meaning of every moment. In our pilgrimage everything is important, everything is a part of it.

There is an oft-quoted line from the first Indiana Jones movie that comes when he finds himself in a dangerous situation. Asked for his plan, he confesses: "I don't know. I'm just making this up as I go along." Our prospects are quite a bit better than that. When God instructs Abraham to get going in Genesis 12, he only points in the right direction, he does not provide a roadmap. (This is discussed more fully in Chapter 5 of *From Fear to Faith.)* Even though *Abraham set out, not knowing where he was going* (Hebrews 11:8), he was not condemned to be an aimless wanderer. A mapless journey means Abraham has to stay open to the future and be listening for directions at every turn in the road. His was a map that unfolded as he journeyed; he has to be on the move in order to learn where he is going.

> Living in the here and now is like driving a car at night, to borrow an analogy from novelist E. L. Doctorow. You drive only as far as the headlights allow. But if you keep driving at the edge of what you see you will eventually make the whole trip. So I try to follow the light I have. And it's enough.[6]

What I like most about my GPS is that it provides the distance to the next turn and if I happen to miss that turn it recalculates and provides the way to get back on the path to the programmed destination. Most helpful, especially when you are driving in Atlanta! It keeps me from despairing or becoming too frustrated with rush hour traffic (which in Atlanta is practically 24/7). Our faith in God's ability and willingness to give us next step or next turn directions, plus recalculation to get us back on track, provides hope during any time but especially during difficult times. No place becomes a dead end. Detours become expected and acceptable parts of the journey

Psalm 23:3 is usually translated: *He guides me in paths of righteousness* or *He guides me in right paths.* Rabbi Harold Kushner translates it: *He guides me in straight paths for His name's sake*, then notes that the Hebrew literally means *roundabout ways that end up in the right direction.* He comments: "Maybe in plane geometry the shortest distance between two points is a straight line. But in life the shortest distance to our goal may be an indirect, roundabout route."[7]

We may even find ourselves experiencing what Abraham and Sarah experienced:

> Abraham and Sarah are models, called as they were to leave the Fertile Crescent for desert places unknown. "Saddle up, we're moving out." "Where are we going?" "I'll tell you when we get there." And they went out, marching off the map of what they knew as the civilized world.[7]

Although I never developed it, I thought an interesting sermon subject might be "Marching Off the Map." The point of the sermon would be that we march off the map we have into the unknown but we never march off God's map. Sub-points in the sermon would deal with our limited perspectives and inadequate knowledge. Our pilgrimage may often find us in unfamiliar territory, unfamiliar to us but not to God. Wherever we find ourselves - in Oz or Wonderland or other places unknown - we maintain faith that God has not abandoned us. Unlike Jacob who exclaimed, *"Surely the Lord is in this place - and I did not know it"* (Genesis 28:16), we need to affirm at all points along our journey, "Surely the Lord is in this place - and I know it!"

What About Progress?

No parent traveling with a child can count the number of times the question came, "Are we almost there?" My response was usually, "No, but we are travelling in the right direction." We will deal more with this in Chapter 10 but, in life as well as on a trip to Disney World, the most important thing to note is that you are headed in the right direction. This lowers the frustration level during times of traffic congestion, road construction, and posted detours. My confession is that progress in my personal spiritual journey has been much slower than I had expected. I thought that at this point in life I would be much further along the road to maturity. Much comfort has come from a prayer I remember going something like this: "I'm not all I should be, I'm not all I could be, and I'm not all I'm going to be. But, thank God, I'm not all I used to be!" Once when responding to some criticism, I responded, "This is the best I've ever been."

Being patient with ourselves is a necessary ingredient in our own pilgrimage as well as that of others. Another necessary ingredient: "The first lesson for enduring happiness is this: Celebrate your progress."[8] Celebrating what we have accomplished, how far we have come, the changes we have made - all contribute to a healthier and more positive approach to life. We'll deal later with some of the shadow stuff (Chapter 7), but for now I want to underscore the importance of intentionally celebrating your progress – regardless of how little it may seem to be.

> What does a snail say when riding on the back of a turtle? "Whee!"[9]

Even when you feel like a snail on the back of a turtle, you need to shout "Whee!" Who cares how many others are in the fast lane? Why do we keep comparing ourselves with super saints? Who cares if others are light years ahead of us? We won't forever be progressing at a snail's or turtle's pace but sometimes that is the best we can do. So celebrate your progress, if not in miles, then in inches. To inch your way along means you are still moving in the right direction.

Four quotations provide a good summary of this section:[10]

> Let's face it, it is only progress if you are moving in the right direction.
>
> Practice doesn't make perfect. Practice makes progress.
>
> We must never allow our spirit to be stifled by failure. Failure is a part of progress, not a final outcome.
>
> I have not had much experience with being perfect, but I had had considerable experience with making progress.

Laughing Pilgrims

It has never failed. The times when I have taken myself too seriously are those times in which I have gotten into the most trouble. In *Laughing Pilgrims: Humor and the Spiritual Journey,* Howard Macy offers this bit of wisdom:

> Laughing at our own klutziness makes a lot of sense. Probably you've noticed that arrogance stifles humor. It's hard to laugh when you're ten feet above contradiction. Accepting the fact of limitation also frees us to be playful, to enjoy the world more fully.[11]

I have finally learned that living even a few feet above contradiction is not an option, even if I wanted to. Much has been written about humor as a moderator of life stress. A physician has a lecture that includes his famous prescription, "Take two laughs and call me in the morning." We often speak about how grief unites us but there is also the healing and unifying power of laughter. And because tears and laughter are so close to one another, I hardly ever conduct a funeral service without an appropriate reference to some humorous incident in the life of the deceased. (These references are supplied by members of the family and are used with their permission.) No one wants to be remembered as living ten feet above contradiction.

Some are amazed to discover that Freud viewed jokes as an important means by which we save in "psychical expenditure."

> In a little-known article titled "Thoughts for the Times on War and Death" (1915), Freud observes that we humans tend to live beyond our psychic means....Humor saves the expenditure of three forms or expressions of psychic resources. These are *painful emotions, costly inhibitions,* and *difficult thinking.* He suggests a link between jokes and an economy in the expenditure of costly inhibitions, and between the comic and an economy in the expenditure of difficult thought or ideas.[12]

In one church, things were going so badly that in our staff meetings we began to talk about "the bomb of the month";

Murphy seemed to be working overtime in all our endeavors. This didn't mean we simply dismissed our efforts with a casual brush of "Oh, well." We did try to learn from our mistakes and remain in dialogue with our congregation. Things did get better. I did not have this quote at the time, but it was relevant in that and many other situations:

> The humor of absurdity enables one to cope with a situation in which we might otherwise lash out in a hapless gesture of revenge, succumb to a helpless sense of fear, or yield to a mood of hopeless despair. The title of a book by Paul Watzlawick, *The Situation is Hopeless, but Not Serious* (1983), expresses the idea that through the gift of a humorous attitude, one may experience a sort of triumph in what are clearly dire circumstances.[13]

I am not suggesting that tragedy, calamity, and evil be summarily dismissed with a grin. Absolutely not! I am not suggesting that we can laugh our way out of everything. There is certainly a time to weep with those who weep (Romans 12:15). There is a time to mourn (Ecclesiastes 3:4). There is no place for inappropriate (misplaced) humor. There is no place for caustic or put-down humor. There is no place for humor at someone else's expense.

Most of the persons with whom I have had serious conflict have been those who did not possess much of a sense of humor. In one church where I was doing an intentional interim, my wife was seated at a table with one of those "serious" persons. In the course of our discussions, I was using humor quite freely.

Somewhere along the way, this person turned to my wife and asked, "Is he always this silly?" to which Pat responded, "No. Sometimes he's worse." I worked with this congregation for almost two years and I don't remember ever seeing her smile. I suspect her life had been colored by circumstances that continued to be a dark shadow over her existence - even as a Christian. She did not find it possible at this juncture of her journey to be a "laughing pilgrim."

Every Journey Has an End

Barbara Brown Taylor writes about the observance of Lent, which for earlier Christians "was set aside for the greening of the soul, which began with penitence and fasting." Lent begins forty days before Easter with Ash Wednesday, named for the imposition of ashes on the forehead:

> For the rest of the day people will look quizzically at our faces, and a few will helpfully tell us that we have dirt on our foreheads. Although I have never actually done it, I have been tempted to say, "Yes, I know. That's my mortality. I thought I'd let it show today."[14]

Ernest Becker didn't need to write *The Denial of Death* to let us know of the most forbidden subject in America. Sex and money have moved from the margins of polite conversation to center stage but death has never reached an acceptable or comfortable level except for memorial services where the emphasis is always on the celebration of life. This continues to be my emphasis but it does not come at the denial of death or the failure to acknowledge our mortality. It shows whether we intend for it to or not.

A human skull on the desk of a philosopher can still be seen in some older paintings. It was there as a reminder of the brevity of life and the need to make every day count with full and intentional living to the highest possible level. Volumes have been written about the necessity of facing our own mortality in order to be able to fully invest in living. Every life has an ending, every journey has a final destination. That is not pessimism or doom and gloom or negative thinking. It is the most basic tenant of Reality 101.

> The Christian doctrine of the Last Things is always affirming the one great truth, through all its varied imagery, namely, that the only true evaluation of this world is one which recognizes the impermanence of this world. Here we have no abiding city; we seek one that is to come, beyond history and beyond death. We are always strangers and sojourners; our citizenship is in Heaven.[15]

Biblically speaking, we are talking about the new heaven and the new earth of Revelation. We are talking about the consummation of history, the triumph of truth and righteousness and grace and love, the final judgment and destruction of evil – all that distorts and attempts to destroy God's intention for life and his universe. Many sophisticated believers cringe at the thought of singing "This world is not my home, I'm just a passing through; My treasures are laid up somewhere beyond the blue," but the truth of our "predicament" has never been more clearly stated.

I'll never forget the line I heard from a minister on October 10, 1966. It impressed me so much that I wrote it down and filed it away. It came from a worship service on the radio. The choir had just finishing singing one of the great hymns of faith and the minister began his sermon with these words: "We're on our way to heaven and enjoying the trip!"[6] It is such a temptation to travel as the Hebrew children did in the wilderness – griping and grumbling and complaining every step of the way. Many seem to have never been able to appropriate Jesus' promised gift for themselves: *"I have said these things to you so that my JOY may be in you, and that YOUR JOY may be complete"* (John 15:11, emphasis mine).

In an early sermon on life as pilgrimage, I used the analogy of life often feeling like an old Saturday matinee movie serial. The end of each chapter was a cliff-hanger; the situation appeared to be utterly impossible; we didn't see how our hero or heroine could possibly be rescued. But we knew they would make it because they had completed all twelve episodes (chapters) of the series. God has written the last episode for all of us - it is the open gate of the Kingdom. He has committed himself to seeing us all the way through the journey to the very promised end – which turns out to be an entirely new beginning (Revelation 21 and 22). We are pilgrims but we will finally arrive.

[1]Kathreen Norris, *Acadia & Me* (New York, Riverhead Books, 2008), 142-143.

[2]Diamuid O'Murchu, *Quantum Theology* (New York, Crossroad Publishing, 2004), 46.

[3]Brenning Manning, *The Relentless Tenderness of Jesus* (Grand Rapids, Revell, 2008), 43.

[4]William Shakespeare, *As You Like It,* Act II, Scene VII, Line 141f.

[5]William Shakespeare, *The Tragedy of Macbeth,* Act V, Scene V, Line 24f.

[6]Timothy Jones, *Awake My Soul* (New York, Doubleday, 1999), 61.

[7]W. Paul Jones, *Trumpet at Full Moon,* 77.

[8]Matthew Kelly, *Perfectly Yourself,* 26.

[9]Donald Capps, *A Time to Laugh: The Religion of Humor* (New York, Continuum Publishing, 2005), 60.

[10]Matthew Kelly, *Perfectly Yourself,* 11, 12, 19, 21.

[11]Howard Macy, *Laughing Pilgrims* (Waynesboro, Ga., Paternoster Press, 2006), 25.

[12]Donald Capps, *A Time to Laugh,* 8-9.

[13]Ibid, 23.

[14]Barbara Brown Taylor, *Speaking of Sin* (Boston, Cowley Publications, 2000), 73.

[15]J. S. Whale, *Christian Doctrine* (Cambridge, University Press, 1966), 176.

[16]Dr. Williams, Bible Way Church, Washington, D.C.

Searching for a Metaphor for Life
Points to Ponder

A far more hopeful metaphor is one that can be found in almost every culture: the metaphor of life as a journey.

In our pilgrimage everything is important, everything is a part of it.

A mapless journey means Abraham has to stay open to the future and be listening for directions at every turn in the road. His was a map that unfolded as he journeyed; he has to be on the move in order to learn where he is going.

In life, the shortest distance to our goal may be an indirect, roundabout path.

Our pilgrimage may find often find us in unfamiliar territory—unfamiliar to us but not to God.

Unlike Jacob who exclaimed, *"Surely the Lord is in this place – and I did not know it"* (Genesis 28:16), we need to affirm at all points along our journey, "Surely the Lord is in this place – and I know it!"

The first lesson for enduring happiness is this: Celebrate your progress.

It has never failed. The times when I have taken myself too seriously are those times in which I have gotten into the most trouble.

The Christian doctrine of the Last Things is always affirming the one great truth, through all its varied imagery, namely, that the only true evaluation of this world is one which recognizes the impermanence of this world.

Chapter 3: You Have to Believe in Endings and Beginnings

MODERN OBSERVATIONS:

The main reason we get trapped in the helplessness state is that we let ourselves become fixed and set into one role, function, work, or relationship and expect that never to become obsolete.[1]

Maybe God's Hall of Fame is like baseball's, filled with superstars who got on base only once in every three attempts.[2]

"I consider every loss in life as the throwing off of an old garment in order to put on a new one: and the new garment has always been better than the old."[3]

We cannot live the afternoon of life according to the programme of life's morning – for what was great in the morning will be little at evening, and what in the morning was true will at evening have become a lie.[4]

A man met an old college friend downtown one night. They sat in the lobby of the hotel and began to talk over old times. Before they realized it, it was long past midnight. They each went home a little fearful of what their wives would say about their coming in so late. The next day they met again. One asked, "How did your wife take your coming in so late?" "Oh," the other replied, "I explained it to her and it was all right. What about your wife?" "Well," he said, "when I came in my wife got historical." "You mean hysterical, don't you?" his friend asked. "No," he said, "I mean historical. She brought up everything that has happened the past thirty years." (Source unknown.)

THE BIBLICAL TEXT: Philippians 3:12-14:

> *Not that I have already obtained this or have already reached the goal; but I press on to make it my own, because Christ Jesus has made me his own. Beloved, I do not consider that I have made it my own; but this one thing I do: forgetting what lies behind and straining forward to what lies ahead, I press on toward the goal for the prize of the heavenly call of God in Christ Jesus.*

The Past is What it Is

As I work on the first draft of this chapter, we are in the closing days of 2011. The year is almost gone. For many its events are forever fixed; the past is so final. These words from Omar Khagyam come to mind:

> The moving finger writes: and having writ moves on: nor all thy piety nor wit shall lure it back to cancel half a line nor all thy tears wash out a word of it.

In one sense, this is true – but it's not from Holy Scripture. It doesn't offer much hope about the past or the future. The biblical text from Philippians 3:12-14 does not deny the reality of what has been but it provides an entirely different perspective on what has been called "the march of time." Through the years I have preached several different sermons using this same text:

1. "Letting Go of the Past in Order to Claim the Positives of the Future."
2. "You Don't Have to Stay Down."
3. "It Is Never Too Late to Begin Again."
4. "Reframing the Past in Order to Live in the Present and Have Hope for the Future."
5. "Great Resiliency."

Once when I was working on a sermon from the above text, I made a mistake I didn't catch until I reread it. Instead of typing *forgetting what lies behind* I typed *forgetting what lives behind.* What a Freudian slip of the fingers! In Book II of his *Confessions,* Augustine maintains:

> Strictly speaking, there is no past, present, or

> future, but rather a past present, a present present, and a future present. The past is no more, and the future is not yet, except as it is held in our memories.[5]

In an early pastorate, I was visited by a man who came to see me about what he termed his "problem." It was our first meeting and he looked a little disheveled. I had already heard that he was the kind and gentle neighborhood alcoholic. He wanted me to do something for him. His wife had left him and he wanted her to come back; he asked if I would talk to her for him. Something he said raised a question in my mind and I asked, "How long has she been gone?" He replied, "Fifteen years!" I said very calmly, "I think she's probably decided to stay gone." The way he told the story it sounded as though she had been gone a week.

In a later pastorate, I was visited by a woman who wept as she told the account of her husband having an affair and "running off" with another woman. I had learned before her visit that this had occurred ten years earlier. I listened more sympathetically to this story than I had to the one told me many years earlier. What I have learned through the years is that the past is with us and cannot be denied. We are all products and, too often, prisoners of the past. Many things were quite painful, hurtful, and downright harmful. The past has left its mark on us with both physical and emotional scars. Complexes, prejudices, and defenses plague us; much of which we are almost totally unaware.

Philip Yancey gives these brief paragraphs on the late Henri Nouwen, who is perhaps best known for his book *The Wounded Healer*:

> A defining characteristic of Nouwen: he does not spare himself or his readers the embarrassment of truth, no matter how bad that truth makes him look. Much suffering, Nouwen said, stems from memories buried deep inside, which release a form of toxin that attacks the center of one's being. Good memories we display in the form of trophies, diplomas, and scrapbooks; other painful memories remain hidden from view, where they escape healing and cause enduring harm.
>
> Our instinctive response to such wounding memories is to act as if they did not happen, to not talk about them and think instead of happier things. But by the deliberate act of not remembering we allow the suppressed memories to gain strength and maim our functioning as human beings. Nouwen had the courage to shine the light on some of those dark places, to expose the wounding memories within himself. "The only true healing," he said in a memorable phrase, "is a wounded healer."[6]

Paul never suggests that he ignores what is behind him; his letters refer to things for which he has deep regret. We can't change the past but we have a great deal to do with how much power it has over us.

The Great Transition

A writer tells of reciting a long series of woes to a

counselor friend who listened for a long time. Then the counselor took a cassette tape and said, "On this tape are three short recordings made by three persons who came to me for help. They are not identified, of course. I want you to listen to the recordings and see if you can pick out the two-word phrase that is the common denominator in all three cases." The writer could not spot the phrase and was told, "Perhaps that's because you used it three times yourself in talking with me....They are the two saddest words in any language – 'If only.'...The trouble with 'if only' is that it doesn't change anything. It keeps the person facing the wrong way – backward instead of forward. It never gets out of the past tense. The remedy is...to change the key words and substitute a phrase that supplies life instead of drag." The writer asked, "Do you have such a phrase to recommend?" His counselor friend said, "Certainly. Strike out the words 'if only'; substitute the phrase 'next time.'" [7]

"If only" is a dead end street; "next time" is a new lease on life. Paul's "next time" is the phrase *straining forward to what lies ahead, I press on.* It is Paul's affirmation of a new beginning. Proverbs 26:16 proclaims the necessity for new beginnings (in the plural): *for though they (the righteous) fall seven times, they will rise again.* Believing in endings and beginnings is the commitment to make great resiliency one of the major traits of your life. The New Living Translation renders Paul 's *(we are) struck down, but not destroyed* (II Corinthians 4:9): *We get knocked down, but we get up again and keep going.* One of the great secrets of the "successful" life is not never getting knocked down, it is not staying down.

Our hope is not that we will never fail, slip, or fall. Our hope is expressed plainly in this prayer from Andrew Greeley:

> Why is my spiritual life always about getting back on course? Why does every new onslaught of effort and responsibility, even pleasant effort and rewarding responsi`bility, sweep me away from the Spirit? Because I'm human, I guess.
>
> I'm sorry that I'm always beginning again after a lifetime of trying, but also grateful for the grace you give me to begin again...I (really do have) faith in the second chances. I do believe...that. I...know it is true from the experiences of life. One must be willing to start over again. Each day. Like today.[8]

I vividly remember seeing somewhere a cartoon about the prodigal son. A huge table is loaded with tons of food. An older man in eastern dress is talking with a much younger man standing at his side looking at the feast. The caption reads: "Now son, I want you to remember, this is after all the fourth fatted calf." This brings more than a smile to my lips, it brings joy to my heart because the possibility pictured here is what keeps me going. Many have observed: "No measuring line has ever been invented that can fix the limits of grace." If I believed grace had limits I would never have the courage to get up after having fallen; I would never have the courage to move from "if only" to "next time."

One of my real treasures is a devotional book titled *God Calling,* edited by A. J. Russell but authored simply by "Two Listeners." I have been reading it daily for over fifty years. One of my favorite readings is for August 20. Here is an excerpt:

> And so now today, I say to you...that you are not to dwell for one moment on your sins, your mistakes, and faults, and bad habits of the past. You must be as one who runs a race, stumbles and falls, rises and presses on to the goal. What avails it if he stays to examine the spot where he fell, to weep over the delay, over the shortsightedness that prevented his anticipating and avoiding the obstacles? So with you, and I lay it on you as a command – no looking back. Give yourself, and all you ever met a fresh start from today.[9]

The Great Reluctance

Not all endings have to do with moving on from painful or negative experiences. Many endings in life have to do with acknowledging what is over and cannot possibly continue into the present. It has to do with the series of losses we all experience in life and the willingness to know when it is time to close out one chapter in our lives and begin another one. This is one of the most difficult things we ever do; some simply refuse to do it.

On May 31, 2009, Huston Smith turned ninety. He wrote a book based on his "reflection upon turning ninety." He titled it *Tales of Wonder.* And nothing is more of a wonder than what he writes about the necessary move to an assisted-living facility:

> The first night after the move was a dark night of the soul. Religion relies on that successful plot device, the happy ending. I still believed in one, but after my first night in the assisted-living

> residence I thought: the happy ending will now have to wait until I am dead. And then after three days here, it became acceptable, perfectly fine. The move seemed no more than turning the page of a book. On the previous page I had been on Colusa Avenue and on this page I am here, but the story itself has not changed. And ninety, I discover, is a good age for making new friends. The maintenance man, Mr. Lin, has just left my room, and how coincidental: he grew up in China near where I grew up! We have wonderful conversations, in Chinese.[10]

Although I am still in my seventies, some chapters have already closed and, thankfully, new ones have begun. Nothing is sadder than the popular song of some years ago with the lines: "Those were the days, my friends, we thought they'd never end. We thought we'd laugh and sing forever and a day." Perhaps that is the way it ought to be. We are not meant to punctuate every festive occasion with the lament, "This can't last." This attitude precludes our entering fully and joyfully into life's great celebrations with family and friends. Later in life we have to find new celebrations. Again, Huston Smith:

> People go to nursing homes, I've heard it said, to die. I came to this assisted-living residence, it seems, to cheer people up. I still begin each day with exercise for the body, reading religious classics for my mind, and prayer for the spirit....I have added a fourth practice. Mentally I take a census of the other residents here, and as each

appears in my imagination, I ask how I might improve his or her day.[11]

It is to be noted that Huston Smith mourned for three days the closing of the former chapter of his life. He faced the reality of a significant and unalterable change in his life. Something was over - never to return. He did not deny reality but then he decided not to hang his harp on a weeping willow tree. He decided that wherever he was and however he was there was a purpose and plan for his life - as long as it lasted. That is the most significant decision any of us can ever make. I do believe that *in everything God cooperates with us for good* (Romans 8:28). That certainly doesn't mean that everything that happens to us is good - some of it is just terrible. Tragedies are not shrugged off with a simple "whatever God wills I will accept." People who say things like that usually don't!

It is a great temptation to assume that the place where we are right now is not the place to live. It's not so much the decision to die as it is the decision to hold back, to refuse to reach out, to deny ourselves the joy of existence that our Lord promised to us - regardless (see John 15:11). Huston Smith found others in the assisted-living residence who had come there to die. He chose not to be among that number. Who can sing the Lord's song in a foreign (strange) place? We can. It's simply another one of those faith decisions.

[1]Wayne Oates, *The Struggle To Be Free* (Philadelphia, Westminster Press, 1983), 127.

[2]Philip Goldberg, *Roadsigns on the Spiritual Path* (Boulder, Sentient Publications, 2006), 152.

[3]Elizabeth Lesser, *The New American Spirituality* (New York, Random House, 1999), 291.

[4]Sue Monk Kidd, *The Heart Waits*, 9.

[5]Quoted in Charles Pinches, *A Gathering of Memories* (Grand Rapids, Brazos Press, 2006), 137.

[6]Philip Yancey, *Soul Survivor* (New York, Doubleday, 2003), 304.

[7]Arthur Gordon, *A Touch of Wonder* (New York, Revell, 1974), 76-78.

[8]Andrew Greeley, *Sacraments of Love* (New York, Crossroad, 1994), 162.

[9]A. J. Russell, ed., *God Calling* (New York, Dodd, Mead, & Co., 1945), 163.

[10]Huston Smith, *Tales of Wonder* (New York, HarperOne, 2009), 177-179.

[11]Ibid, 180.

You Have To Believe in Endings and Beginnings
Points to Ponder

The main reason we get trapped in the helplessness state is that we let ourselves become fixed and set into one role, function, work, or relationship and expect that never to become obsolete.

What I have learned through the years is that the past is with us and cannot be denied.

By the deliberate act of not remembering we allow the suppressed memories to gain strength and maim our functioning as human beings.

We can't change the past but we have a great deal to do with how much power it has over us.

Strike out the words "if only"; substitute the phrase "next time."

One of the great secrets of the "successful" life is not never getting knocked down, it is not staying down.

No measuring line has ever been invented that can fix the limits of grace.

Many endings in life have to do with acknowledging what is over and cannot possibly continue into the present.

Huston Smith found others in the assisted-living residence who had come there to die. He chose not to be among that number.

Part I: What Time Is It?
Reflections

At the conclusion of a workshop I did on Baptist history, one of the participants quipped, "I didn't know Baptist history could be so entertaining!" I just smiled but what I wanted to say was, "Why not?" I confess the use of much humor in my Bible studies and workshops; it has certainly been one of my survival strategies. Some books immediately jump off the shelf as I pass by. Such was the case with *Laugh Your Way to Grace* by Susan Sparks. The subtitle: *Reclaiming the Spiritual Power of Humor.*[1] The back cover states:

> Laughter was honored by the ancients as a spiritual healing tool and celebrated by the world's great religions. So why aren't we laughing along the spiritual path today? What would happen if we did?

Through her book I became aware of the American Dialect Society that picks a word of the year. In 2003, inspired by Governor Arnold Schwarzenegger and his movie character *Terminator,* "governator" was the chosen word. Stephen Colbert contributed "truthiness" as the winner in 2005. Spark's favorite came in 2006, the year in which the International Astronomical Union decided that Pluto would be downgraded from a planet to a dwarf planet. From that came the termed *plutoed,* meaning "devalued." What a great word to describe so many things we have always depended on and were certain would last – at least as long as we do.

Perhaps this word for 2006 has really been the word for every year; we just didn't want to admit it. The exiles had been plutoed by the Babylonians and Paul and Silas had been plutoed by the Roman authorities. The exiles were solely tempted to live as the devalued; Paul and Silas never saw themselves in that way. Retirement fund losses, unemployment, a failed business venture, interruption in education plans, unexpected responsibilities, a failed marriage, a frightening medical diagnosis, betrayal by a friend, disruption in family relationships, and a host of other unforeseen occurrences can all cause one to feel plutoed.

While not a simple panacea, the accepted metaphor of life as pilgrimage -with the unexpected a natural part of the journey and the continuing necessity of recognizing endings and beginnings - can go a long way toward helping us learn to live in difficult times. As I look back over my years of ministry, I never found saying "goodbye" to be easy. Saying, "This chapter is over," was never a simple matter. Sometimes I had to be pushed to acknowledge that something was over. But I never failed to discover (even in the most painful conclusions) that something new was about to begin.

Somewhere I read that one of the secrets of getting the most out of life is being willing to live fully the age you are. In an old radio show, one man talked about his wife's attempt to recapture her youth. His friend's comment was: "It's going to be pretty hard to capture anything that got away that long ago." Some things are over – never to be recaptured. But there are things to be captured at our present age, at this present juncture in our lives. Wonders are meant to unfold all along the way. Look for them especially at the time of painful loss and transition. Believe that the words of Psalm 40 are meant for you: (Revised English Bible):

Patiently I waited for the Lord;
he bent down and heard my cry.
He raised me out of the miry pit,
out of the mud and clay;
he set my feet on rock

and gave me a firm footing.
On my lips he put a new song....

[1]Susan Sparks, *Laugh Your Way to Grace* (Woodstock, Skylight Paths, 2010).

Part II: Maintaining Mountaintop Perspectives

Chapter 4: On Being A Game Changer

MODERN OBSERVATIONS:

In today's world, traditional scientific values such as determinism and predictability yield pride of place to openness and creativity.[1]

What were they thinking when they named the alarm clock? Why not call it the opportunity clock?[2]

Grace claims the future as its peculiar domain. Grace declares itself whenever the plot seems at a dead end. It is the story for anyone who thinks his or her story has already ended. (Comments on the story of Ruth.)[3]

We have to be as hard-headed as possible about reality and possibility.[4]

You can't stop the waves, but you can learn to surf.[5]

Walter Brueggemann¨ "Fixity is not a quality of serious reality."

THE BIBLICAL TEXT: Exodus 32:9-14:

The Lord said to Moses, "I have seen this people, how stiff-necked they are. Now let me alone, so that my wrath may burn hot against them and I may consume them; and of you I will make a great nation."

But Moses implored the Lord his God, and said, "O Lord, why does your wrath burn hot against your people, whom you brought out of the land of Egypt with great power and a mighty hand? Why should the Egyptians say, 'It was with evil intent that he brought them out to kill them in the mountains, and to consume them from the face of the earth'? Turn from your fierce wrath; change your mind and do not bring disaster on your people. Remember Abraham, Isaac, and Israel, your servants, how you swore to them by your own self, saying to them, 'I will multiply your descendants like the stars of heaven, and all this land that I have promised I will give to your descendents, and they shall inherit it forever.'" And the Lord changed his mind about the disaster that he planned to bring on his people.

Different Biblical Points of View?

A couple of years ago I preached a sermon on the above text and titled it: "Is the Future Open or Do You Simply Need a Crystal Ball?" I write this next sentence clearly aware of how controversial it is. You know it's a big question when even biblical writers can't agree on it and different points of view are clearly presented. This needs considerable unpacking.

Some Scriptures make it sound as though God has a detailed future plan for each of us and we can't help very much what we are destined to live out. Other Scriptures tell us that the choices we make and the actions we take largely determine what the future holds for us.

For instance, in Isaiah 14:27 we are told: *The Lord Almighty has spoken – who can change his plans?* And in II Kings 20:1-6 we have the story of God's sending Isaiah to king Hezekiah with this message: "*This is what the Lord says: set your affairs in order, for you are going to die. You will not recover from your illness.*" A few verses later, God commands him to return to the king with an updated message: *"I have heard your prayer...and I will add 15 years to your life."* This appears to be a change of plans if ever I have heard it – a change of plans on God's part in response to Hezekiah's prayer.

Ecclesiastes 6:10 tells us: *Everything has already been decided. It was known long ago what each person would do. So there's no use arguing with God about your destiny.* When we get to chapter 9 and verse 11, we are told: *It's all decided by chance, by being in the right place at the right time.*

Numbers 23:19 seems all too clear: *(God) is not a human, that he should change his mind.* And so does Exodus 32:14: *And the Lord changed his mind about the disaster that he planned to bring on his people.*

If all this is not confusing enough, we have a couple of other biblical indicators about the future. In Joel 2:14, the prophet tells the people: *Who knows? Perhaps even yet (the Lord) will give you a reprieve, sending you a blessing instead of this terrible curse.* "Who knows" and "perhaps" don't sound very much like fixity in the future. The question really is as old as time: Is every play in the great game of life already predetermined, or is it possible to be a game changer?

The Word That Won't Go Away

In light of conflicting biblical texts, a couple of observations need to be made. Toward the end of his life, Thomas Aquinas, the great Christian theologian, had a dream. In it, he was trying to empty out the ocean with a teaspoon. When asked by a student what he was doing in his dream, Aquinas replied, "Theology."[6]

Alongside this I place these two sentences from a more contemporary theologian: "Beginners in theology frequently expect to read works of Christian thought as if they were reading Agatha Christie. It may require wit to read Ms. Christie, but it does not require courage. Theology requires courage."[7] Heeding this challenge, we are going to approach the text from Exodus 32 with courage and with our minds in gear as we do biblical theology.

The context of this episode is all important. While Moses is up on the mountain communing with God and receiving the Ten Commandments, the people are in the valley getting restless. When the days turn into weeks and the weeks turn into more than a month, the people complain to Aaron that Moses may have died on the mountain talking to this invisible God and they need some kind of a god they can see in order to make it through the rest of their journey. Aaron responds by receiving their gifts of gold and fashioning the infamous golden calf. The people build an altar and offer sacrifices.

The Lord commands Moses to get down off the mountain because: "*YOUR people have acted perversely*" (emphasis mine). God further informs Moses that he intends to unleash his wrath upon the people and begin anew with him in creating a new nation. Moses pleads with God on behalf of the people. Some translations tell us that *the Lord relented*...but It carries the same meaning as our translation: *the Lord changed his mind.* In other words, the future is now different from what it might have been because of the intercession of Moses.

For those who contend that they are not theologians, I beg to differ. Whenever you talk about your faith, your belief in the nature and purposes of God, how you view life, what you think about the future, what you believe to be your calling in life, etc., you are doing theology. I would challenge you to do biblical theology because, if you spend most of your time on the biblical mountaintops, the future is filled with hope and possibility.

Victims or Choosers?

It has always seemed rather strange to me that some people feel more secure if they believe the future is fixed and there's not much they can do about it except find out what it will be and try their best to cooperate with the inevitable.

A boy is standing beside his father's armchair as the dad looks at his son's clearly unsatisfactory report card. The cartoon's caption reads: "What do you think the problem is, Dad? Nature or nurture?" Either way the son if off the hook! To use a favorite current phrase: "It is what it is!"

If the cartoon's question is correct, then all of us are simply in the category of victim and our single reply to those who question us is, "I couldn't help it! I'm not responsible because it's just in the cards I've been dealt." Aside from being a fatalistic point of view, this attitude ignores everything it means to be created in the image of God. It ignores everything about choosing and deciding. Also, why is God going to bother to have a judgment day and hold us accountable if we simply can't help it?

There remains in our culture a great fascination with horoscopes and the words of psychics because there lurks the belief that the future is already shaped out ahead of us. Two things I need to say: First, in the Scriptures, prophets are not so much foretellers of the future as those who are "forthtellers." They point out what they believe God is doing in the present and his purpose and will for his people. They talk much about how to live and what will be inevitable if the people do not remain faithful to their calling. Second: I do believe that God's ultimate purposes and will cannot be thwarted. That is: God will ensure the final triumph of righteousness, justice, mercy, grace, and love, the destruction of evil and the final redemption of creation resulting in a new heaven and a new earth (Revelation 21).

Ecclesiastes 10:14 is probably the most ignored passage in all the Bible: *Foolish people claim to know all about the future and tell everyone the details! But who can really know what is going to happen?*

One of the current raging debates among theologians involves just how much of the future is open to God and to us. One of my favorite Sufi stories is the following:

> To the disciples' delight the master said he wanted a new shirt for his birthday. The finest cloth was bought. The village tailor came in to have the Master measured, and promised, by the will of God, to make the shirt within a week.
>
> A week went by and a disciple was dispatched to the tailor while the Master excitedly waited for his shirt. Said the tailor, "There has been a slight delay. But, by the will of God, it will be ready tomorrow."
>
> Next day the tailor said, "I'm sorry it isn't done. Try again tomorrow and, if God so wills, it will certainly be ready." The following day the Master said, "Ask him how long it will take if he keeps God out of it."[8]

The moral is obvious. The completion of the shirt has nothing to do with God and everything to do with the tailor! There is not a fixed future date for the completion of the work; the future is open and based on what the tailor does.

The Great Partnership

It may sound radical, but we are always a part of the future and so is God. Walter Brueggemann's *An Unsettling God* contains these most unsettling sentences:

> The big idea of this book is that the God of ancient Israel is a God in relationship, who is ready and able to make commitments and who is impinged upon by a variety of "partners" who make a difference in the life of God....This suggests that the defining category for the faith in the Old Testament is dialogue, whereby all parties - including God - are engaged in dialogic exchange that is potentially transformative for all parties....including God."[9]

This would be an unthinkable concept of God if it were not contained in Holy Scripture. (Just as the nature of God as revealed in the Incarnation is unthinkable without it!) Moses engages in dialogue with God and the future is different for the children of Israel because God responds to Moses' intervention. Dialogue is not only a part, but is integral to Old Testament faith.

God tells Moses that his wrath is red hot and he is ready to consume the people and start over again with him. Moses pleads with God to think about this action that would certainly give the Egyptians the last laugh. Moses pleads with God to remember his promises to Abraham, Isaac, and Jacob. And God LISTENS to Moses and changes his mind about what he is going to do.

Quantum theory has upset some people because it "represents the micro world of subatomic particles as sheer randomness and indeterminacy." Commenting on this principle, an author writes:

> Randomness becomes an important way in which God's providence is at work in secondary causality....If God has created a world so thoroughly shot through with indeterminacy and chance, then God risks much by making a world so open to possibility.[10]

I have often wanted to tell people who are concerned about knowing the future: "Don't look into a crystal ball; hold your two hands in front of you and look at them. You'll see more clearly the future there than anywhere else."

I conducted the funeral service for a woman whose printed obituary in the local newspaper contained these lines:

> Toward the end of her life when she lost the ability to walk, she grieved for about 24 hours before deciding that she would adapt productively and joyfully to her capabilities. On the afternoon preceding her death, Mrs._____ entertained a bridge club at her new home of a few months (an assisted-living facility) where it is reported that her partner and she had their highest score in two years.

My observation is that she decided to live all the days of her life – whatever came and wherever the location. The bottom line for Mrs.____ and the bottom line in this chapter is that we do not have to live as victims of a preprogrammed destiny. What we do makes a difference in the world. We are the most important ingredient in our futures.

But, of course, not in isolation. We need to remember Paul's great prophecy about the future in Romans 8:28: *in all things God cooperates with us for good.* When we live responsibly in the light of these words who knows what great possibilities the future holds?

Or to phrase it another way, like Moses we can be game

changers in the lives of others; we can certainly be the game changer in our own lives.

[1]David O'Murchu, *Quantum Theology*, 139.

[2]Matthew Kelly, *Perfectly Yourself*, 211.

[3]J. Ellsworth Kalas, *Grace in a Tree Stump* (Louisville, Westminster John Knox, 2005), 69.

[4]Douglas Hall, *Thinking the Faith*, 176.

[5]Jack Kornfield and Christina Feldman, *Soul Food* (San Francisco, HarperSanFrancisco, 1991), 247.

[6]David Wolpe, *Why Faith Matters* (New York, HarperCollins, 2008).

[7]Douglas John Hall, *Thinking the Faith,* 242.

[8]Anthony de Mello, *One Minute Wisdom* (New York, Image Books, 1988), 54.

[9]Walter Brueggemann, *An Unsettling God* (Minneapolis, Fortress Press,2009), xi-xii.

[10]John E. Thiel, *God, Evil, and Innocent Suffering* (New York, Crossroad Publishing, 2002), 135-136.

On Being a Game Changer
Points to Ponder

You know it's a big question when even biblical writers can't agree on it and differing points of view are clearly presented.

Theology requires courage.

Whenever you talk about your faith, your belief in the nature and purposes of God, how you view life, what you think about the future, what you believe to be your calling in life, etc., you are doing theology.

Why is God going to bother to have a judgment day and hold us accountable if we simply can't help it?

The defining category for the faith in the Old Testament is dialogue, whereby all parties - including God - are engaged in dialogic exchange that is potentially transformative for all parties - including God.

If God has created a world so thoroughly shot through with indeterminacy and chance, then God risks much by making a world so open to possibility.

We are the most important ingredient in our futures.

Like Moses, we can be game changers in the lives of others; we can certainly be the game changer in our own lives.

Chapter 5: Truth and Love Belong Together

MODERN OBSERVATIONS:

In a letter to a Roman Catholic (1749), John Wesley wrote: "If we cannot as yet think alike in all things, at least we may love alike."[1]

We can summarize (John) Wesley's views of theological diversity as follows: In essential beliefs, let there be unity. In those things that are not essential, let there be freedom. In all things, let there be love.[2]

The standard translations of I Corinthians 13:4-8 contain a lot of adjectives. The Greek does not contain a single one. Instead we have a mass of verbs, things love does and doesn't do. This is the ultimate authority for saying "Love is a verb."[3]

A good friend pulls us away from our self-defeating and often hopeless attitudes. A good friend gives advice, but as Samuel Taylor Coleridge stated, the advice is like snow. The softer it falls, the longer it dwells and the deeper it sinks into the ground.[4]

A good friend is one who opens the door a crack and lets light into the room.[5]

Tell all the Truth but tell it slant...
Too bright for our infirm Delight
The Truth's superb surprise!
The Truth must dazzle gradually
Or every man be blind.
— Emily Dickinson

THE BIBLICAL TEXT: Ephesians 4:14-16:

We must no longer be children tossed to and fro and blown about by every wind of doctrine, by people's trickery, by their craftiness in deceitful scheming. But speaking the truth in love, we must grow up in every way into him who is the head, into Christ, from whom the whole body, joined and knit together by every ligament with which it is equipped, as each part is working properly, promotes the body's growth in building itself up in love.

Some Things Are Not Up for Vote

In going through my files, I found this quote from Leonard Nolt:

> ...if the people in the Bible had voted, at least some of the time, it would have led them away from God. Can you imagine what the election results would have been if Moses had called for a vote to find out what the Israelites wanted to do when they were caught between the Red Sea and the pursuing Egyptians? How many would have voted to step into the Red Sea?

Although God has given us freedom and the right to make decisions for ourselves, sometimes I don't believe God cares what we think. There are some things where God simply has the first word that is also the last word. He is not waiting or encouraging us to wait on the results of a popular vote.

I believe the reason for this is two-fold. First, there are some things that are right and voting doesn't affect the rightness of them one way or another. It doesn't matter how we feel about them or vote on them. There are great moral principles that God has set in his universe and they are not subject to my approval. Second, some of these things that are right are so frightening that to put them into practice is almost like stepping into the Red Sea. We fear that we will immediately be in over our heads, never realizing that the moment we step in, God will make a way through.

In the above text, Paul (we will not deal with the controversy over authorship) is giving material he wants the church at Ephesus to discuss at their next business meeting. He gives them some information about the way things are. Then he tells them how they are to live in the light of the way things are. This is a text about church unity and the only way there can be unity. This is a text about church growth; it is a different kind of church growth than most of us have ever heard about but it is the kind of church growth the New Testament preaches on every page.

This text is the challenge to go forward with what Paul is convinced to be God's command just as surely as it was God's command for the children of Israel to go through the Sea. I'm convinced it's just as frightening for us as it was for them. I'm also convinced it is the only way to go.

One of Paul's Paradigms

I once did a sermon series titled "Paul's Paradigms." *Truth and Love Belong Together* is one of those paradigms. The phrase can be variously translated: *speaking the truth in love* (New Revised Standard Version); *maintain the truth in the spirit of love* (Revised English Bible); *speak the truth with the accent of love* (William Barclay).

A cursive reading of this passage might suggest that Paul's major concern is correct doctrine. He has been on enough stormy seas to know what it means to be tossed about by wind and waves. He warns his friends: *We must no longer be children, tossed to and fro and blown about by every wind of doctrine....*But that is not all he says and I maintain it is not the major emphasis of the passage. The emphasis is on the strong connection between love and truth. Paul Tillich advised that we distrust any claim of truth where we can observe the lack of love.

Those who lived through the ugly battles between warring factions in the Southern Baptist Convention may not be aware of a statement by W. A. Criswell: "I wish that the people who believed the most about the Bible had the most loving spirit about what they believed, me included. The war of words must have grieved our loving Father, for it certainly broke my heart."[6] There was probably enough lack of love to encompass far too many of those involved in the controversy. It has never been easy for those who hold deep faith convictions to keep truth and love together.

A story circulated about a young man studying cello under the great master, Pablo Casals. The student cited a practice session in which he played a difficult piece with great precision. "I knew I had played it flawlessly and I was looking for high praise from the master who had been listening very intently. Instead, I heard him say, 'You are playing the notes, but not the music.'" The all too obvious application to our text is: Paul would warn that we may have the notes of truth but if we do not have love, we are not playing the music. And if we don't have the music, what is the purpose of the notes? In I Corinthians 13, Paul is so radical as to say that regardless of what else we may have, if we don't have love, we have nothing. Except, he is much harsher than that; without love he says we are nothing.

The Recipe for Honesty With Style

Some people pride themselves on giving you the unvarnished truth. They come like great truth bulldozers, whether it is truth in the area of faith or truth in the area of your personal life. Unfortunately, bulldozing truth often destroys far more than it can ever help rebuild. In a chapter titled "The Right Truth at the Right Time," (some of the ideas in this final section come from this chapter) Lewis Smedes writes:

> Some people believe that we should tell the truth for truth's sake. They tell everything they know as soon as they hear it, tell it to anyone within earshot, no matter what it is. They use truth like a machete. They slice their way through people and leave them bleeding in the spillage of sacred truth. The bloodshed is sanctified by the sacredness of truth.
>
> But a person of integrity does more than tell people what is on his mind. He learns the art of telling the truth well. To tell it with love – helpfully, healingly, even though painfully – this is the skill that turns honesty into art.[7]

Smedes then cites Aristotle's recipe for honest with style:

The right truth...
To the right person...
At the right time...
In the right way...
For the right reason.

Not every truth is mine to tell. Just because I can say, "Well, it's true," doesn't mean it should be shared. Where did we ever get the idea that people have "the right to know"? (This is not the same issue as "freedom of the press." It's probably time to resurrect "all the news that's fit to print" and add "all the news that fit to hear.") For instance, should the newspaper obituaries always include the cause of death? If your response is "yes," I simply ask, "Think about it." Speaking the truth in love may mean that sometimes (often?) love calls me to remain silent. If the truth will only add hurt or pain or further damage relationships, why should I tell it?

> What is mine to tell? The truth that helps someone who needs it, this is the truth that is mine to tell. The truth another person needs in order to make a free decision, this is the right truth to tell....So is the truth that keeps an intimate relationship honest, or makes a sad person laugh, or reveals a beauty or a mystery that someone may never see If it is not told. And, more than anything, the truth to tell is the truth that another person is loved and forgiven, accepted, beautiful, and worthy.[8]

Jesus did not give his disciples all the truth they needed to hear. *"I still have many things to say to you, but you cannot bear them now. When the Spirit of truth comes, he will guide you into all truth"* (John 16:12-13a). My interpretation of this text is that the Spirit continues to guide us into truth a small portion at a time, as we are able to assimilate and use it. "Tell me the truth," should be rephrased, "Tell me the amount of truth I am at this present moment able to hear and use constructively without being crushed."

Jesus was sensitive to how much of the truth the disciples could appropriate. Nobody has the right to back up a dump truck load of truth and let you have it. It will bury you! Even if it is all truth and even if they say they are doing it because they really care. If they really cared they would keep the dump truck at home and bring over the truth a thimble full at a time. Jesus promised that the Spirit would guide his disciples into greater truth just as he had done.

I have often thought of the way Jesus must have told Peter the truth about his coming denial. You remember that with the trial and crucifixion fast approaching, Jesus tells his disciples they will all deny him. Peter immediately assures his Lord that even if all the others betray him, he will remain faithful. Does Jesus say, "There you go, boasting again! So over confident!"? Does he then point a finger and lecture, "Listen, you big lummox, I tell you this very night before the rooster crows you will have denied me three times"?

Or - does he look at Peter with genuine love and affection and quietly say to him, "Peter, I tell you, this very night before the rooster crows you will have denied me three times." This latter approach is certainly characteristic of the way Jesus addressed himself to all the weak, injured, and fallen humanity he encountered. This truth expressed in any other way could have destroyed Peter.

Truth for the Right Reason

Lucy and Charlie Brown are standing at the wall
- usually a philosophical moment.:

> Lucy: Are you interested in having me tell you something for your own good?
>
> Charlie Brown: I'm not sure.
>
> Lucy: Well...if it will help you to make up your mind....I'd enjoy it, too!

That is too often the real reason someone is anxious to tell us the truth! And, of course, it is the wrong reason. The right reason is given in our text:

> ...speaking the truth in love, we must grow up in every way into him who is the head, into Christ. (We must speak the truth that) promotes the body's growth in building itself up in love.

Are we to grow up in speaking the truth or are we to grow up in love? I think the text is plain and concur with this commentary: "This growth is to be in love which goes better with the verb to grow up than with speaking the truth."[9]

Most people don't need more truth. Most of us have more of that now than we can handle. Most of us need more love (and to give more love). No one wonders why Jesus gave what many have called the eleventh commandment: "*I give you a new commandment: love one another; as I have loved you, so you are to love one another. If there is this love among you, then everyone will know that you are my disciples*" (John 13:34-35).

It is not just that we have his truth but that we have his love. When we love as he loves us, then we will share the truth so that it heals and helps and builds-up and strengthens. Even when that truth must confront, we will do it in a way that is constructive, not destructive. When truth and love go together, we can learn the art of telling the truth well. This is the way to turn honesty into art: the right truth to the right person at the right time in the right way for the right reason.

I told you this text was like stepping into the Red Sea. Almost everybody gets nervous when you put love ahead of truth. When Paul completes his famous chapter on love (I Corinthians 13), he does not say, "Make truth your aim." He admonishes, *"Make love your aim"* (I Corinthians 14:1). I don't believe there is any question about it. Truth and love do belong together – but love always has to be a step or two out in front.

My wife's favorite critique of some of my prognostications is, "Take them out of the box." Meaning: unpack them, explain them, make them concrete and specific. When I say that love and truth belong together, the kind of love I'm talking about is I Corinthians 13 kind of love; it is not squishy or sentimental, it is pro-active, creative, and redemptive. Let me spell out the fifteen positive and negative aspects Paul attaches to *agape* (the Greek word for love he chooses):

1. Love is patient. The word describes patience with people, not with circumstances. It is used of God himself in his relationship with human beings.[10]
2. Love is kind. *Love looks for a way of being constructive* (Phillips translation).
3. Love is not envious.
4. Love is not boastful. *Love makes no parade* (Moffatt translation).
5. Love is not arrogant. Love is not inflated with its own importance. *Love gives itself no airs* (Moffatt translation).
6. Love is not rude. *Love has good manners* (Phillips translation).
7. Love does not insist on its own way. *Love does not pursue selfish advantage* (Phillips translation).
8. Love is not irritable. *Love is not touchy*

(Phillips translation).

9. Love is not resentful. Love does not keep a record of wrongs received. The word used is the Greek word for entering an item in a ledger so that it will not be forgotten.[11]
10. Love does not rejoice at wrongdoing. When someone says to you, "I know you'll be sorry to hear this about so and so," and you feel within, "On the contrary, I'll be delighted to hear it," then you know that love has flown out the window.
11. Love rejoices in the truth. *There is nothing love cannot face* (Revised English Bible).
12. Love bears all things. *Love knows no limit to its endurance* (Phillips translation).
13. Love believes all things. *Love is always eager to believe the best* (Moffatt translation).
14. Love hopes all things. Love never ceases to hope.
15. Love endures all things. *Love never gives up* (Today's English Version).

"When the world and judgment say 'This is the end,' love alone can see the way out.'"[12]

[1]Charles Yrigoyen, Jr., *John Wesley* (Nashville, Abingdon Press, 1996), 6.

[2]Ibid., 97.

[3]Sarah Ruden, *Paul Among the People* (New York, Pantheon Books, 2010), 180.

[4]Robert Veninga, *A Gift of Hope* (New York, Ballantine Books, 1985), 64.

[5]Ibid., 162.

[6]Reported by Timothy George in *Christianity Today,* March 11, 2002.

[7]Lewis Smedes, *A Pretty Good Person* (New York, Harper & Row, 1990), 79-80.

[8]Ibid., 81.

[9]*Broadman Bible Commentary* (Nashville, Broadman Press, 1970), XI, 158.

[10]William Barclay, *The Daily Study Bible: Corinthians* (Philadelphia, Westminster Press, 1956), 133.

[11]Ibid. 136.

[12]Morton Kelsey, *Reaching* (San Francisco, Harper & Row, 1989), 16.

Truth and Love Belong Together
Points to Ponder

Although God has given us freedom and the right to make decisions for ourselves, sometimes I don't believe God cares what we think. There are some things where God simply has the first word and the last word.

Some of the things that are right are so frightening that to put them into practice is almost like stepping into the Red Sea.

We are to distrust any claim of truth where we can observe the lack of love.

Bulldozing truth often destroys far more than it can ever help rebuild.

Nobody has the right to back up a dump truck load of truth and let you have it.

Most people don't need more truth. Most of us have more of that now than we can handle.

This is the way to turn honesty into art: the right truth to the right person at the right time in the right way for the right reason.

Truth and love do belong together – but love always has to be a step or two out in front.

Chapter 6: Are You Doing Anything Exceptional?

MODERN OBSERVATIONS:

Christian discipleship is a very dangerous thing.[1]

People should be able to see in us what God is like.[2]

(Jesus') first recorded miracle was at a wedding in a Galilean town called Cana. He made one hundred and eighty gallons of wine for people who'd already been drinking; John tells us that "*he thus revealed his glory, and his disciples put their faith in him* (2:11).[3]

For much of my life I would have been the indignant disciple: "*Why this waste? For this ointment might have been sold for a large sum, and given to the poor*" (Matthew 26:8-9). Jesus' response is special. She has done "*a beautiful thing to me*" (v. 10).[4]

The first conviction that has become a prize for me is this: To be human at its best is to make mutual covenants with other people and to keep them faithfully.[5]

Getting our pride and avarice out of the way in deference to the neighbor's well-being goes against the human grain, but that is the shift in outlook. That is the Christian's Copernican revolution.[6]

THE BIBLICAL TEXT: Matthew 5:43-48:

> *"You have heard that it was said, 'You shall love your neighbor and hate your enemy.' But I say to you, Love your enemies and pray for those who persecute you, so that you may be children of your Father in heaven; for he makes his sun rise on the evil and on the good, and sends rain on the righteous and on the unrighteous. For if you love those who love you, what reward do you have? Do not even the tax collectors do the same? And if you greet only your brothers and sisters, what more are you doing than others? Do not even the Gentiles do the same? Be perfect, therefore, as your heavenly Father is perfect."*

The Buzzer Sounds

Many years ago, a movie was advertised as being so shocking that before certain scenes that might cause the weak to faint, a buzzer would sound so that the squeamish could close their eyes. (If that same standard were used today, for many movies the buzzer would never stop sounding.) I mention this because we can easily hear a warning buzzer when we read the above text; it is so outrageous that we want to shut our eyes. It is not for the weak or those who easily faint.

Martin E. Marty once wrote, "Every year I let one book change my way of thinking and living." He does not protect himself from books that challenge and disturb. The very texts that challenge and disturb us ought not have built-in buzzer sounds that cause us to close our eyes. With eyes wide open we need to see and hear texts that may change our way of thinking and living.

Jesus challenges his disciples to be those who are into the "more." J. B. Phillips' translation has provided our chapter title: *Are you doing anything exceptional?* Why would Jesus issue such a challenge?

> Linus and Charlie Brown are having one of their serious discussions.
>
> Linus: I think the world is much better today than it was, say, five years ago.
>
> Charlie Brown: How can you say that? Don't you ever read the papers? Don't you ever listen to the radio? How can you stand there and tell me this is a better world?
>
> Linus: I'm in it now!

Jesus said this world is to be a better place because his followers are in it. His followers are to bring a new dimension to life. *"You have heard it said"* or *"Everybody does it," "But I say to you....*" Not the general ethic, but his ethic. Not simply the civil, courteous way, but the extraordinary way of the more than others. An ethic that makes his followers the salt of the earth and the light of the world (our calling). A part of this ethic means being so exceptional that we act in loving ways even toward our enemies. (See the preceding chapter on the 15 characteristics of Paul's I Corinthians 13 kind of love.)

Not Drudgery, But a Joy

Harry Emerson Fosdick told the story about his mother sending him to pick a quart of raspberries. He didn't want to do it. He reluctantly dragged himself to the berry patch in rebellion. Then he had a revolutionary idea. It would be fun to pick two quarts of raspberries and surprise the family. That changed everything. He said he loved picking the raspberries![7]

This is the story of the duty of the first mile and the joy of the second. In the Sermon on the Mount, Jesus challenges us: *If anyone forces you to go one mile, go also the second mile* (Matthew 5:48). A Roman soldier could force a citizen to carry his pack a mile. That was an obligation. The victory that would leave the soldier open-mouthed in surprise, was the offer to carry it the second mile. The first mile keeps you captive and submissive; the second mile is grace and freedom. Another one of Jesus' great paradoxes where the first are last and the last are first.

When Jesus tells us, *"My yoke is easy and my burden is light"* (Matthew 11:30), we wonder how that can be with requirements such as this one. Once you begin to live in the exceptional, you are set free to live in joy. Life literally takes wing. You are no longer captive to others or to life. With all the current uproar about the posting of the Ten Commandments in public places, I like to remind people that the Gospel of Matthew presents Jesus as the new Moses and it is not accidental that early in the Gospel we are told: *Jesus went up the mountain, and after he sat down, his disciples came to him. Then he began to speak, and taught them saying...*(Matthew 5:1-2). The usual custom in the synagogue was for the rabbi to stand for the reading of Scripture and be seated when he began his official teaching. Here in Matthew is the new Moses on a new mountain teaching about Kingdom living based on a new covenant that was to be ushered in with the death and resurrection of the long awaited Messiah.

The problem with legalism is its inherent question: "What are the requirements?" The liberating quality of grace is that ethics becomes the response of gratitude. The motivation is not one of avoiding judgment and condemnation, but one of increasing gratitude for the enlarging possibilities of life lived on a grander scale. Picking the second quart of raspberries, going the second mile, acting in a loving way toward our enemies is not just about what we do – it has everything to do with the kind of persons we become. Although not the reason for doing what Jesus asks because it shifts the focus to us, a corollary of adherence to this kind of behavior always results in our feeling better about ourselves! Getting even with enemies may result in momentary satisfaction, but none of us really admire the kind of person who is into revenge. We see plenty of examples of the results of the "eye for an eye and tooth for a tooth" philosophy; if carried to extremes, eventually the world becomes populated with the blind and the toothless! We may get even, but at what a price.

Instructions on Loving Enemies

A footnote in the Revised Standard translation of Matthew 5:44 tells us: some late manuscripts add *bless those who curse you, do good to those who hate you and pray for those who persecute you.* (These additions are found in Luke 6:27). This has nothing to do with love being the way you feel but love being the way you act. We can't help how we feel; we can control what we do. Here is a simple formula for loving the *agape* way as Jesus commands:

1. Bless. Don't curse, don't get out a voodoo doll,

don't give anyone the "evil eye."

2. Do good. Actions are to be constructive, not destructive.
3. Pray for.

We can do all of these exceptional things whether we feel like it or not. Emotions are not the issue and, anyway, you can't be commanded to feel a certain way. Instructions can be issued for behavior – that involves a choice on our part.

The inevitable question is: "If I do all this what will be the results?" There is an old saying, "If you will be nice to people they will be nice to you." Not necessarily! Sometimes it only seems to give license for new opportunities for their taking advantage of you. Loving your enemies is no guarantee that they will become your friends. This is not the test of your loving. (Sidebar: Some relationships are full of poison and danger. Doing the three things Jesus advocates does not mean staying in close proximity to the enemy. Do you remember the rabbi's response in *Fiddler on the Roof* when asked if he has a blessing for the Czar? He pauses for a moment and responds, "May God bless the Czar and keep him far away from us!" Not a bad blessing in that situation!)

Matthew 5:45 states the results of being extraordinary in our loving: *so that you may be children of your Father in heaven.* It has always seemed significant to me that the two ways in which Jesus said we can show we are his followers are both connected with love. The first is the above mentioned and the second is found in John 13:34-35: *Just as I have loved you, you also should love one another. By this everyone will know that you are my disciples, if you have love one for another.* I wonder what the Christian world would look like if our major contest was trying to out-love one another? I wonder what my ministry would have looked like if in every situation I had made it my first priority to love all the members of my congregation the way Jesus loves me?

Most agree that *love your enemies* is the one unique saying of Jesus on love. There was no precedent for it. When you read the Gospel stories, you discover that Jesus got into the most trouble by practicing what he preached. He demonstrated love to the unacceptable and unlovable of his day. Not only tax collectors and other "sinners," but especially Samaritans were drawn within the circle of his love. It is difficult to imagine the uproar caused by responding to the question: "Who is my neighbor?" with a story that has a Samaritan as its hero and example of what it means to be neighbor.

When we do the exceptional thing in the realm of love, Jesus says we are marked off as belonging to him. I can't think of any better motivation.

And If That's Not Bad Enough

Our above discussion does not represent the only area in which Christians are to be exceptional. I just couldn't close this chapter without mentioning another one found in I Corinthians 6:1-8:

> *When any of you has a grievance against another, do you dare to take it to court before the unrighteous, instead of taking it before the saints? Do you not know that the saints will judge the world? And if the world is to be judged by you, are you incompetent to try trivial cases? Do you not know that we are to judge angels – to say nothing of ordinary matters? If you have ordinary cases, then, do you appoint as judges those who have no standing in the church? I say this to your shame. Can it be that there is no one among you wise enough to decide between one believer and another, but a believer goes to court against a believer – and before unbelievers at that?*
>
> *In fact, to have lawsuits at all with one another is*

> *already a defeat for you. WHY NOT RATHER BE WRONGED? WHY NOT RATHER BE DEFRAUDED? (emphasis mine). But you yourselves wrong and defraud – and unbelievers at that.*

There is no way I have the space (or the knowledge!) to deal with all this text contains. We will confine ourselves to buzzer sounding admonitions right up there with *love your enemies.* It is indeed being exceptional when you find a situation in which it is better for all concerned to let someone take advantage of you. Paul is not talking about becoming a doormat or having no point of view or assuming the role of victim. He is advocating what many modern writers have said in other ways:

> "It is a sign of maturity to give in occasionally." (Frank Kostyu).
>
> "Do you know that the ready concession of minor points is a part of the grace of life?" (Henry Harland).
>
> "If you watch...you will see...that almost all church fights and splits occur because people do not have the freedom to give in to each other."[8]

Several things in the context of the times contribute to a better understanding of what Paul is asking. The Jews did not ordinarily use the public law courts. Rabbis cited Exodus 21:1 as the reason for not taking a case before a pagan judge. Usually, three judges were appointed from the synagogue or local community to handle disputes. By contrast, the Greeks found the law courts to be one of their chief amusements and entertainments. In Athens, a highly complex judicial system was developed involving sometimes as many as six thousand citizens on a jury![9]

It appears that some in the church at Corinth were taking such matters as property grievances before these pagan courts. (Paul is not talking about criminal cases.) For the sake of the witness of the Gospel and the health of the Christian community, Paul asks this shocking question: Why not sometimes rather be wronged and cheated when there are bigger issues at stake? Think of the price you pay if you live this way. Somewhere I found this:

> It's like the story of a doctor who put a patient on a strict diet that was to increase his chances for a longer life. After a couple of months, he asked the man how the diet was going. The patient answered, "It's working. Life seems longer already!"

Many things that are right and good for us and others are really tough. Often they seem to go against the natural flow of things. Who wouldn't choose a banana split over a serving of spinach? Answer: someone who is keeping an eye on the bigger picture.

Paul says it is better for a Christian to be wronged than to wrong, to be defrauded than to defraud. As someone is reported to have said, "I'd rather be the person who bought the Brooklyn Bridge than the one who sold it." Plato maintained that a good person always chooses to suffer wrong than to do wrong. The bottom line: I must be more concerned about my responsibilities than my rights. In the culture of our day, this sounds both exceptional and extraordinary.

The Forgotten (and Somewhat Hidden) Command

In the King James' version, Jesus' response to the woman who anoints his head with expensive ointment is : *she has wrought a good work upon me* (Matthew 26:10). A better translation is: *she has done a beautiful thing to me.* The same Greek word is used in Matthew 5:16 which is usually translated: *...let your light shine before others, so that they may see your good works and give glory to your Father in heaven.* Again, the better translation is: *let your light shine before others, so that they may see your beautiful works and give glory to your Father in heaven.*

Matthew 5:20 warns: *For I tell you, unless your righteousness exceeds that of the scribes and Pharisees, you will never enter the kingdom of heaven.* If you have any knowledge of just how good these groups were, you are left wondering how this could ever be possible. I used to see labels in supermarkets of escalating quality: "our good quality"; "our better quality"; "our finest quality." Jesus is calling for righteousness of the finest quality. No one could ever deny that the Pharisees were good; hardly anyone would have labeled their goodness beautiful. It was not winsome and attractive to those inside the Jewish tradition, much less to those outside the faith.

Few would deny that there never was a person whose goodness exceeded that of Jesus. What is most striking about that goodness is that it was magnetic to those the Pharisees marked as sinners. I once preached a sermon on Matthew 7:15-23 titled "Is Your Christianity Beautiful?" People are never won over by a righteousness that is mean and ugly. One of the tests as to whether we are doing anything exceptional might be to ask if our goodness is beautiful. A good discussion question: why was Jesus welcomed into the homes of the "sinners" and outsiders of his day? (More about this in Chapter 9.) Few "sinners" appear to have been won over by the righteousness of the scribes and Pharisees.

Jesus' command to us is to be those whose righteousness is marked by the exceptional and the beautiful.

[1]Joan Chittister, *New Designs* (Erie, Benevision, 2002), 11.

[2]Ibid., 73.

[3]Paul Coughlin, *No More Christian Nice Guy* (Minneapolis, Bethany House, 2005), 34.

[4]W. Paul Jones, *Trumpet at Full Moon,* 144.

[5]Wayne Oates, *The Struggle To Be Free,* 144.

[6]Gaylord Noyce, *Why Can't I Believe?* (St. Louis, Chalice Press, 1999), 34.

[7]Harry Emerson Fosdick, *The Secret of Victorious Living* (New York, Harper & Brothers, 1934), 2.

[8]Richard Foster, *Celebration of Discipline* (San Francisco, Harper & Row, 1978), 97.

[9]*Broadman Bible Commentary,* X, 322.

Are You Doing Anything Exceptional?
Points to Ponder

With eyes wide open we need to see and hear texts that may change our way of thinking and living.

The first mile keeps you captive and submissive, the second mile is grace and freedom.

The problem with legalism is the inherent question: "What are the requirements?"

Getting even with our enemies may result in momentary satisfaction, but none of us really admire the kind of person who is into vengeance.

Loving your enemies is no guarantee that they will become your friends.

When we do the exceptional thing in the realm of love, Jesus says we are marked off as belonging to him.

If you watch you will see that almost all church fights and splits occur because people do not have to freedom to give in to each other.

Who wouldn't choose a banana split over a serving of spinach? Answer: someone who is keeping an eye on the bigger picture.

I must be more concerned about my responsibilities than my rights.

No one could ever deny that the Pharisees were good; hardly anyone would have labeled their goodness beautiful.

Reflections on Part II: Maintaining Mountaintop Perspectives

An ever-present temptation in the Christian faith is to major on the minors, and minor the majors. I know this is true because I have done it far too many times. I have to keep asking myself, "Is there a larger issue at stake? Is there something of more importance I need to consider? Am I standing on a biblical mountaintop when I take my stand on this issue?" Paul Johnson's observation is instructive:

> What did Jesus teach? He had no system, no summa, no code. God forbid! The only way to grasp his teaching is to read all the Gospels repeatedly, until its essence permeates the mind.[1]

In Bible studies, I will contend that we can never say, "Well, I'm through with the Gospel of John." The reason? The Gospel of John will never get through with us! That can be said of the Bible as a whole. There is no way we can ever exhaust the richness of Scripture or claim that all its truths have taken hold of our lives. I am amazed at how many new things I find as I continue reading all the Bible. Many times in the past I have glanced over books and passages that didn't seem to have much to offer; I now find that I missed many things I desperately needed to hear.

While not ignoring any part of Scripture, I have always preached that we need to have our minds shaped and receive our marching orders from the biblical mountaintops. The emphasis in Jesus' teaching, the way he related to all people, his constant challenge to those who wanted to limit God's grace, his unwillingness to erect any boundary between himself and others, the extraordinary way he spoke and acted – all are a challenge to much of the restricted thinking and living of many of his followers in our time.

And, alas, in too much of my time in pastorates. I remember with shame an incident with a rural congregation. In a deacon's meeting, we were discussing possible locations for a church office. Several possibilities were offered and then the strongest voice in the group (the one who usually won the debates) suggested that the office be in the attic section over the present small Sunday School office. He paused and offered, "Of course, it will be awfully hot in the summer and, because there is no heat up there, it will be awfully cold in the winter." I immediately spoke up and said, "That the dumbest suggestion I've heard!" It was not the dumbest thing of the day. The dumbest thing that happened that day was my response to the deacon's suggestion. My words may have been true (we didn't locate the office there) but they were not pastoral in any sense of the word. I stepped way down in the valley to come up with that zinger.

Maintaining the mountaintop perspectives of Jesus will always be a challenge to the popular religion and culture of the times. It is what brought the condemnation and wrath of the established Christian community down on most of those we today regard as "Saints." Sometimes it's called "coloring outside the lines" but I prefer to see it as coloring INSIDE the lines Jesus established in his teaching and healing ministry. The Gospels are clear about Jesus' getting into trouble from the very beginning of his public ministry, but most would agree that he got into the right kind of trouble.

In the forward to Henlee Barnette's autobiography, Walter Shurden writes: "...as professor of Christian Ethics at Southern Seminary he would teach thousands of ministers to learn to think biblically and critically, while urging them to act compassionately and courageously."[2] That is not only what he taught, that is the way he lived. I was fortunate enough to be one of the participants in "Barnette's Buddies," a group that met monthly in Henlee's home for dialogue with this retired professor who never retired from life. I have never known anyone quite like him. A good summary of Part II can be found in his words:

> Christianity is a way of life undergirded by faith in God. I once said this in a sermon. A deacon of the church approached me and informed me that he had been a deacon in that church for twenty years and never thought of Christianity as a way of life. Christian ethics demands moral action on all issues that depersonalize humanity. My job, my calling, was – and continues to be while I have breath – to tackle any and all forces that dehumanize God's children.[3]

[1]Paul Johnson, *Jesus* (New York, Viking, 2010), 82-83.

[2]Henlee Barnett, *A Pilgrimage of Faith* (Macon, Mercer University Press, 2004), xiii.

[3]Ibid., 144.

Part III: “In the Meantime” Priorities

Chapter 7: Out Came This Calf

MODERN OBSERVATIONS:

"Nothing is so difficult as not deceiving oneself." Ludwig Wittgenstein.[1]

When we undertake the journey toward wholeness, we need to be on the lookout for that neurotic person that Jung described as one-sided – "someone who overemphasizes one side of his personality to avoid dealing with the other." That person is us.[2]

E. E. Cummings wrote about walking inside "the ragged meadow of my soul." One day I said to my counselor, "Surely one of the hardest things in life is learning not to kid ourselves."

A man called me one afternoon and said, "We've got marriage problems. Can I send my wife to see you?"[4]

THE BIBLICAL TEXT: Exodus 32:19-24:

> *As soon as he came near the camp and saw the calf and the dancing, Moses' anger burned hot, and he threw the tablets from his hands and broke them at the foot of the mountain. He took the calf that they had made, burned it with fire, ground it to powder, scattered it on the water, and made the Israelites drink it.*
>
> *Moses said to Aaron, "What did this people do to you that you have brought so great a sin upon them?" And Aaron said, "Do not let the anger of my Lord burn hot; you know the people, that they are bent on evil. They said to me, 'Make us gods, who shall go before us; as for this Moses, the man who brought us up out of the land of Egypt, we do not know what has become of him.' So I said to them, 'Whoever has gold take it off'; so they gave it to me, and I threw it into the fire, and out came this calf!"*

Tired of Waiting

Moses would probably fare much worse today than he did in the above text. He is a dawdler; most holy persons are. The people Moses has led out of Egypt want a go-getter and Moses has been up on this smoking, shaking, awesome mountain of God for forty days and nights. Most think he's probably died up there.

I can almost hear the murmuring (for which they will later become famous and the model for countless followers through the centuries): "What could be taking so long? If this God who brought us out of slavery has anything to say to us, let him speak up. We've got things to do, places to go, lands to conquer. We've no time to waste."

Aaron responds, "Let me see what I can do." So while Aaron is taking the bull by the horns (pun intended), the dawdler Moses is receiving the Ten Commandments. These are the words Moses is to take down the mountain for the people. In one of the Bible's most disturbing stories, God announces to Moses that the people have made an idol and he has decided to destroy them and start over again in the building of the great nation he promised to Abraham.

Moses pleads for the people (this is discussed more fully in Chapter 4) and Exodus 32:14 records the results: *And the Lord changed his mind about the disaster that he had planned to bring on his people.* Sidebar: in the lives of the saints, the closer they get to God the more loving and compassionate they become.

But even holy people have been known to pitch a fit or two along the way. When Moses gets down to the foot of the mountain, it's a big fit. The great irony is not lost on the biblical writer. We are told that Moses' *anger burned hot* - the same anger (the same words) Moses has just talked God out of up on the mountain. In his throwing fury, Moses breaks the tablets on which the commandments are written; he grinds the calf into powder and forces the people to drink a gold-dust desert shake.

Oft-Repeated Immortal Words

In his adolescent years, my younger son was famous for his responsive comeback in the face of some item discovered in less than sound condition. With the confident assurance that it was a sufficient explanation, he would say, "It just fell off." When Moses asks, *"What did this people do to you that you have brought so great a sin upon them?"*, Aaron's reply is so classic that if you didn't know it was a biblical story you might think it came from Saturday Night Live. He says, "Well, you know, most of us thought something had happened to you and the people didn't have any authority figure and since everybody else has some sort of god they can see, I was just here to be of service. They gave me the gold they were wearing, I threw it into the fire, and out came this calf!"

With tongue in check, frequently I have offered the secret of life as knowing who to blame. Once you have that taken care of, everything else is a piece of cake. You can blame the crowd, the culture, your upbringing (always a favorite), your genes, difficult circumstances, or forces beyond your control. It is the serious and deadly matter of saying, "I'm not responsible for what happened."

This didn't begin with Aaron. It is as old as the Garden of Eden. When God confronts Adam and Eve for eating the forbidden fruit, Adam defends himself with, "Don't blame me; Eve gave me the fruit." Eve takes the same stance with, "Don't blame me; the serpent tricked me." God responds with the most shattering indictment any of us ever hear: "You are both responsible for what you did."

> When Carl Sandburg was presented with a gold medal for history and biography by the Academy of Arts and Letters he said, "We find it momentous that Lincoln used the word 'responsibility' nearly as often as he used the word 'freedom.'" (Robert J. McCracken).

The ratio in usage of those two words today would be weighted heavily on the side of "freedom." Our founding fathers - and mothers - weighed in heavily on the side of "responsibility." They would never have understood freedom as a license to avoid responsibility for what they had done or for what they ought to do. Duty and obligation were natural components of their vocabulary; they were also unafraid to use and apply the word "sacrifice." For them, the good life was made up largely of words most of us seek to avoid.

Aaron gives a clear picture of the background of his now infamous line "out came this calf." "*You know the people, THEY are bent on evil. THEY said to me, 'Make us gods, who shall go before us...we don't know what has become of (Moses)...So I threw the gold THEY gave me into the fire, and OUT CAME this calf! I was just as surprised as you are!*" He confesses two of three items named by Mohandas Gandhi; Aaron seems to have been unaware of the third:

> I have only three enemies. My favorite enemy, the one most easily influenced for the better, is the British Empire. My second enemy, the Indian people, is far more difficult. But my most formidable opponent is a man named Mohandas K. Gandhi. With him I seem to have very little influence.[5]

Sue Monk Kidd confesses: "I...sat in the midst of many selves. The Pleaser, the Performer, the Perfectionist - my trinity of P's."[6] That trinity of P's belonged to Aaron as well. And lest you think I am too judgmental, in the margin of Kidd's book next to that sentence I wrote, "Mine, too!" Aaron must have felt his popularity soar when he steps into Moses' role and provides the people with what they want. Later, both he and Miriam openly confess their jealousy of Moses (Numbers 12). Gauging behavior solely on people pleasing is always the recipe for disaster. "I simply responded to the people's request," is another way of saying, "It's not my fault; I didn't see any other option."

"The Buck Stops Here"

President Harry Truman kept the above motto on his desk in the oval office. It was his great reminder; it ought also to be our great reminder. Regardless of whatever else comes into the picture, the ultimate responsibility for the decisions I make and the actions I take is mine. Paul states in no uncertain terms: *...each of us will be accountable to God* (Romans 14:12). On accountability day (a term I prefer to "judgment day") I will not be given evaluation forms on which I may grade my family, friends, and enemies. I will only be allowed to talk about myself. Every word will be first person and that person will be me.

Elsewhere I have written with heavy emphasis on grace and love. However, there are too many Scriptures, too many parables, to ignore a central fact in Scripture: there will be a time in which we are asked how we did with what we were given. Perhaps this will not be so much the Lord giving us his analysis of our lives as it will be a fulfillment of I Corinthians 13:12: *Now I know only in part, then I will know fully, even as I have been fully known.* For the first time I will be able to see myself as I really am. (I don't believe this will be an "all at once" experience. Most of us can handle reality only in small doses. After all, we will have eternity to "know" ourselves and continue our growth in grace.)

There is a third word I believe should be added to the two we usually hear in response to the question "Is it heredity or environment?" That third word is "choice." Over a decade ago it was reported that a scientist had discovered the gene for shyness. He said he would have discovered it sooner except that it was hiding behind two other genes! (He was serious about the first statement.) Of course, it is all three: heredity, environment, and choice. I am solely responsible for the third which can dramatically alter the other two influences. We do not have to be either genetic or cultural victims. It may be tough, it may color everything, but it does not have to determine everything because we can choose. Surely this is a large part of what it means to be created in the image of God. We are not victims; we are choosers.

Several years ago, Continental Cablevision of Madison Heights, Michigan, had trouble with some of its electronic switching equipment, resulting in X-rated programming being fed into the homes of subscribers who hadn't ordered it. One scandalized customer called a local radio station to say, "It was really awful - we saw it for four hours." You wonder why it took four hours to be scandalized. That could be the awful part! The obvious is all too obvious: the electronic switching equipment may have been at fault but there was a decision-making off switch for the TV. The biblical narrative negates Aaron's explanation of *out came this calf.* In Exodus 32:4 we read: *(Aaron) took what they handed him and made it into an idol cast in the shape of a calf, FASHIONING IT WITH A TOOL.* The question to be asked is: How many things handed to me have I fashioned as though I didn't have a choice?

Browsing in a bookstore, I came across a book for young people titled: *Life As Chance or Life as Choice?* I am convinced that those who believe life is mainly chance (the luck of the draw) will live one way and those who believe life is basically choice will live another way. It's the difference between building life on sand or building life on a rock (Matthew 7:24-27). Aaron fashioned the golden calf, we fashion our lives by the choices and decisions we make. We are responsible for the fashioning.

In my file from a *Homiletics Magazine* of 1999, is an article that cites the saying: "If you want to dig a new hole you don't dig the same hole deeper." The writer then gives techniques to use in turning around your life. The list is headed "if you want to":

1. If you want to be healthy, stop doing those

things that harm you.

2. If you want harmony in your life, stop doing those things that cause discord.
3. If you want a closer relationship with your children, stop doing those things and saying those things that build up walls between you.
4. If you want to rekindle the romance in your marriage, stop doing those things that create animosity and boredom.
5. If you want to live in a close-knit, caring community, stop hiding behind the front door.
6. If you want a spiritual life that fills you up, stop pouring all your energies everywhere but toward God.

I choose. I decide. I am responsible.

[1]Quoted in N. T. Wright, *The Last Word* (San Francisco, Harper San Francisco, 2005), 33.

[2]Elizabeth Lesser, *The New American Spirituality*, 83.

[3]Sue Monk Kidd, *When the Heart Waits*, 94.

[4]David Seamands, *Redeeming the Past* (Colorado Springs, Victor Press, 2002), 25.

[5]Jack Kornfield & Christina Feldman, *Soul Food*, 55.

[6]Sue Monk Kidd, *When the Heart Waits*, 6.

Out Came This Calf
Points to Ponder

Once you have taken care of the matter of who to blame, everything else is a piece of cake.

We find it momentous that Lincoln used the word "responsibility" nearly as often as he used the word "freedom."

For our founding fathers and mothers, the good life was made up largely of words most of us seek to avoid.

Gauging behavior solely on people pleasing is always the recipe for disaster.

Regardless of whatever else comes into the picture, the ultimate responsibility for the decisions I make and the actions I take is mine.

On accountability day I will not be given evaluation forms on which I may grade my family, friends, and enemies.

We are not victims; we are choosers.

The question to be asked is: How many things handed to me have I fashioned as though I didn't have a choice?

I choose. I decide. I am responsible.

Chapter 8: A Difficult, Demanding, But Absolutely Essential Word

MODERN OBSERVATIONS:

Before I am asked to show compassion toward my brothers and sisters in their suffering, (God) asks me to accept his compassion in my own life, to be transformed by it, to become caring and compassionate toward myself in my own suffering and sinfulness, in my own hurt, failure, and need. The degree of our compassion for others depends upon our capacity for self-acceptance. When I am most unhappy with myself I am most critical of others. When I am most into self-condemnation, I am most judgmental of others.[1]

A teasing friend once told me, "If you treated others the way you treat yourself, you'd get arrested."[2]

"You may call God love, you may call God goodness, but the best name for God is compassion." Meister Eckhart (a 15th century mystic).[3]

"Whatever God does, the first outburst is always compassion." Meister Eckhart.

One of the most shocking contradictions in Christian living is the intense dislike many disciples of Jesus have for themselves....Through experiencing the relentless tenderness of Jesus, we learn first of all to be gentle with ourselves.[4]

I believe that forgiveness in the teaching of Jesus is not for the sake of moral purity; it's quite simply for the sake of a future.[5]

THE BIBLICAL TEXTS: Hosea 6:6; Matthew 9:35-36; Luke 6:36; James 2:13:

> *For I desire mercy, not sacrifice, and acknowledgment of God rather than burnt offerings.*
>
> *Then Jesus went about all the cities and villages, teaching in their synagogues, and proclaiming the good news of the kingdom, and curing every disease and every sickness. When he saw the crowds, he had compassion for them, because they were harassed and helpless, like sheep without a shepherd.*
>
> *Be compassionate, as your Father is compassionate. (Revised English Bible).*
>
> *For judgment will be without mercy to anyone who has shown no mercy; mercy triumphs over judgment.*

Ubiquitous in the Gospels

In typing the title of this chapter, I made a Freudian slip that was promptly underlined in red. The pre-corrected title: A Difficult, Demanding, But Absoulutely Essential Word. If there is one word that makes up the soul of the Gospels it is the word "compassion." Here is a sample listing (parallel usage is omitted):

> Matthew 9:36; 14:14
> Matthew 18:27
> Mark 1:41
> Matthew 15:32
> Matthew 18:33
> Matthew 20:34
> Mark 5:19
> Mark 9:22
> Luke 7:13
> Luke 10:33
> Luke 15:20

Defining compassion is no simple task. We begin with this word of warning:

> Compassion has to include judgment and all the catch-phrases about "non-judgmental compassion" are a sentimental gloss on the Gospels. Vast harm is done by the refusal to exercise judgment, just because it makes you feel good."[6]

In Hebrew and Aramaic, the word translated "compassion" comes from a word that in its singular form means "womb." Compassion is both a feeling and a way of living that results from that feeling. It literally means "to feel with." It is to identify with another at the deepest level.[7]

> Most commonly compassion is associated with feeling the suffering of somebody else and being

> moved by that suffering to do something. That is, the feeling of compassion leads to being compassionate.
>
> Quite often the Hebrew words for *compassion* and *compassionate* are translated into English as *mercy* and *merciful.* But compassion is quite different from mercy, and being compassionate quite different from being merciful. In English *mercy* and *merciful* most commonly imply a superior in relationship to a subordinate, and also a situation of wrongdoing: one is merciful toward somebody to whom one has the right (or power) to act otherwise. *Compassion* suggests something else. To paraphrase William Blake, mercy wears a human face, and compassion a human heart.[8]

One thing that can be said for certain: "What (Jesus) tried to show was that compassion had, quite literally, no limits."[9] The word used for compassion in Matthew 9:36 is the strongest word for compassion in the Greek language. Except for the parables Jesus tells, it is used only to describe Jesus; it describes all of his acts. As the perfect revelation of the Father, he perfectly lived out Psalm 145:8: *The Lord is gracious and compassionate, slow to anger and rich in love* (New International Version). Compassion is divine; we see it in the Father and we see it in the Son. (Big Sidebar: Compassion IS something you can see!)

A New Way of Seeing

William Willimon wrote the following in an issue of *The Christian Century:*

> Walking across the Duke Campus one fall afternoon during the "Octoberfest," with

> hundreds of students - semi-clothed, many inebriated - carousing and rock music blaring everywhere, my friend Stuart Henry turned to me and said, "Do you know what is for me the ultimate proof of the divinity of Jesus?"
>
> What a strange question, I thought, at this time, in this place. "No, Stuart, what is for you the ultimate proof of Jesus' divinity?"
>
> "It is that statement from the Scriptures that reminds me of how differently than I he views all this; the verse that says '*He looked upon the multitudes and had compassion.*'"

Repeating, this quote from Matthew 9:36 uses the strongest word in the Greek language for compassion. Jesus believed in compassion and felt compassion resulting in a compassionate vision. Before beginning his public ministry he lived for thirty years. Have you ever wondered what he did all those years? He worked in Joseph's carpenter's shop. He mixed and mingled with the people of Nazareth. All we know of those years is that *as Jesus grew he advanced in wisdom and in favor with God and (people)* (Revised English Bible). He laughed at festivals and weddings and wept at times of distress and funerals...including the funeral of Joseph. The word really did become flesh and dwell among us (John 1:14). Rubbing shoulders with us and sharing real life in a real world (a difficult world in Roman-occupied Israel). And because he did, he could look at the multitudes and have compassion.

In a cartoon, a small boy, holding a report card, is facing a distraught parent. The word "underachiever" appears on the card. To this accusation the boy replies, "The problem is not that I'm an underachiever. The problem is that you're an overexpecter." Jesus was not an overexpecter! He saw people as sheep in desperate need of a shepherd. He saw people as *bewildered and dejected,* as *harassed and helpless,* as filled with *weariness and fatigue.* No shepherd was ever an overexpecter when it came to his assessment of his sheep. He knew what would happen if they were left on their own. He knew what would happen to them if they did not have a shepherd.

Matthew tells us that of all the things Jesus could have felt for foolish, wandering, straying sheep, the thing he felt for them was compassion. Jesus felt that way because he knew what they needed. We do not always view people through compassionate lenses. One of my filed articles from 1980 discusses Anita Bryant's divorce after twenty years of marriage to Bob Green. It was especially traumatic because of her crusading efforts against "the disintegration of the American family." She said that the breakup of her family was the most painful experience she had ever encountered. What was even more painful was the reaction of segments of the Christian community that had supported her. All her Christian concerts were cancelled; she received much criticism from Christians. The saddest statement in the article is this one: "Since filing for divorce, Miss Bryant has been in seclusion in Selma, Alabama, with her four children."

Henri Nouwen speaks to this kind of judgment:

> Compassion can never coexist with judgment because judgment creates the distance, the distinction, which prevents us from really being with the other. Much of our ministry is pervaded with judgments. Often quite unconsciously we classify our people as very good, good, neutral, bad, and very bad. These judgments influence deeply the thoughts, words, and actions of our ministry....And so, much of our ministry is limited by the snares of our own judgments. These self-created limits prevent us

> from being available to people and shrivel up our compassion.[10]

Risky Compassion

The way of compassion has usually seemed strange, impractical, and has often proved risky. The religious leaders of Jesus' day could neither stand or understand it. In the midst of their murmuring about Jesus' eating with sinners (the subject of the next chapter), he tells three simple stories about a lost sheep, a lost coin, and a lost son. The key word in these stories is in Luke 15:20: *But while he was still far off, his father saw him and was filled with compassion; he ran and put his arms around him and kissed him.* Compassion for one who with arrogance and pride had left home. Compassion for one who broke the moral law in his loose living. Compassion for one who broke the ritual law in his feeding of pigs. Compassion that puts the signet ring back on his finger and welcomes him back into full legal sonship.

The older brother isn't the only one who can't stand this demonstration of compassion. The Pharisees found it too difficult, too perplexing, too mind-blowing to fit into their system of righteousness. Most remember the scandals associated with the now defunct PTL Club. In Jim Baker's book *I Was Wrong,* he tells what happened to him immediately after his fall: "One of the first people to call was Dr. Billy Graham. I was shocked to hear his voice. Dr. Graham let me know he and his family cared and were praying for me." It is not surprising to find this line in *The Preacher and the Presidents:* "More than anything else, Billy Graham gave Lyndon Johnson what he most craved: love without strings."[11] (Sidebar: Johnson became the first sitting president to attend a Graham crusade, when he appeared at the final service of Graham's ten-day Houston revival in November, 1965.)[12]

Graham created an uproar when, less than two months after the Monica scandal broke, he appeared on the *Today* show and said, "I forgive him. I know how hard it is, and especially a strong, vigorous young man like he is; he has such a tremendous personality. I think the ladies just go wild over him." Commenting on that later, Graham noted: "I said one word - forgiveness - and I got all kinds of ugly letters about that...." Graham created further uproar when a few weeks later he attended the seventy-fifth anniversary dinner for *Time* magazine. Everyone who had ever been on the cover of *Time* was in attendance. Former Yankee player Joe DiMaggio declined to take his assigned place at the table with Bill Clinton. Graham volunteered to take his place. "This was the trademark Graham: the more trouble a president was in – Johnson over Vietnam, Nixon over Watergate, Clinton over Monica – the more prepared Graham was to stand publicly by his side."[13] I can't help noting that all of Jesus' dinner parties with outcasts were very public events.

> "I think we've lucked out with Billy Graham," said historian Martin Marty, "because he doesn't seem to have a mean streak in him." Marty divides American Christianity not between liberal and conservative, but between mean and "nonmean."[14]

What Does Compassion Produce?

Compassion has nothing to do with not holding people accountable for their actions or letting dangerous behavior go unchecked. It is not about "anything goes." It is about the stance of those of us who intend to make a difference in our world by being its light and its salt. By demonstrating what we have come to know as Jesus' stance in a world not unlike our own. Did everyone respond to Jesus' compassion with a change of heart, mind, and direction? We know they didn't, but his compassion offered them the opportunity to *metanoia,* repent (his first word in preaching, John the Baptist's first word). "Will this work?" is not the question to be asked. The questions are: "How ought I to view this situation and this person?" "Is there anything I can do to be an agent of redemption and reconciliation?"

And there is another important question:

> Understanding – compassion – is the foundation of a monastic lifestyle. Without it there is no hope at all for developing a community out of strangers.
>
> Life is not perfect and people are not perfectible. Only understanding, only compassion – the ability to bear life with the rest of humanity, whatever burdens the bearing brings – perfects us.[15]

While pastor in a fairly good sized city, controversy arose over a textbook being used in the local schools. The local ultra-conservative ministerial association sent a letter to the governor of the state asking that the book be removed. They cited the phrase "that d--- cat" as the reason for removal; most of us knew it was the photograph of Martin Luther King, Jr. in the book that stirred them to action. The other ministerial group to which I belonged (you need to know that the local Pentecostal minister was also a member of the group) wrote to the governor voicing opposition to this type of censorship. We all signed the letter. The story made the front page of the local newspaper on a Sunday morning. Arriving at church early that day and checking out things for the early service in the sanctuary, a faithful member came tearing down the aisle and confronted me with, "I can't believe my pastor endorses cursing!" To which I immediately responded, "I'm not a member of the John Birch Society!" To which she immediately responded, "Well, I am!"

I have always regretted my self-righteous assault. While not having changed my mind about the issue, I did not handle the situation with compassion. The woman who confronted me was a caring and sincere Christian who honestly believed in the cause of the group to which she belonged. I never took the time to discover all that had shaped her life and the experiences that had brought her to where she was. I did not take the time to put myself in her shoes, to try to understand the way she understood things. Reponses of that type were not the ones that made me into a better minister, or a better person. It is easy to confront and condemn. It is not easy to enter into dialogue (the subject of Chapter 11).

> Saint Catherine of Siena was asked by one of her nuns, "How can I pay God back for all of His goodness to me? How can I give back to God some of the glory for all His kindness, His love, His mercy, His generosity?" Saint Catherine answered, "It won't do you any good to do any more penances. It won't do you any good to build the great church, because God has the whole world as His sanctuary. But I tell you something which you can do to really pay God back for the love He gives you. Find someone as unlovable as you are, and give that person the kind of love that God has given you."[16]

The bottom line is that we should treat others as God has treated us. We have experienced from the Father and the Son compassion and mercy and grace beyond measure. We have not been dealt with according to our sins nor rewarded according to our iniquities (Psalm 103:10). We have found a shepherd who in love and compassion has always sought us when we have gone astray. Who has always poured the healing ointment on our cuts and bruises. Who has brought us again and again back to the fold of safety and comfort...because he is the good shepherd and we are his sheep.

We love because he first loved us (I John 4:19). We look,

feel, and act with compassion because we have received that compassion - and continue to receive it. What other response could we possibly make to all we have received?

[1]Brennan Manning, *The Relentless Tenderness of Jesus,* 70.

[2]Sue Monk Kidd, *When the Heart Waits,* 67.

[3]Ibid., 147

[4]Brennan Manning, *The Relentless Tenderness of Jesus,* 152.

[5]Richard Rohr, *Hope Against Darkness* (Cincinnati, St. Anthony Messenger Press, 2001), 17.

[6]David Martin, quoted in Rupert Shortt, *God's Advocates* (London, Darton, Longman, and Todd, 2005), 157.

[7]After Marcus Borg, *Meeting Jesus Again for the First Time* (San Francisco, HarperSanFrancisco, 1995), 47.

[8]Ibid., 47-48.

[9]Paul Johnson, *Jesus,* 92.

[10]Henri Nouwen, *The Way of the Heart* (New York, Seabury Press, 1981), 21.

[11]Nancy Gibbs & Michael Duffy, *The Preacher and the Presidents* (New York, Center Street, 2007), 118.

[12]Ibid., 121.

[13]Ibid., 321.

[14]Ibid., 344.

[15]Joan Chittister, *Illuminated Life* (Maryknoll, Orbis Books, 2008), 114-115.

[16]Morton Kelsey, *Christo-Psychology* (New York, Crossroad, 1984), 102.

A Difficult, Demanding, But Absolutely Essential Word Points to Ponder

The degree of our compassion for others depends upon our capacity for self-acceptance.

To paraphrase William Blake, mercy wears a human face, and compassion a human heart.

What Jesus tried to show was that compassion had, quite literally, no limits.

As the perfect revelation of the Father, Jesus perfectly lived out Psalm 145:8: *The Lord is gracious and compassionate, slow to anger and rich in love* (New International Version).

Have you ever wondered what Jesus did all those "silent years" in the Gospels?

Jesus was not an overexpecter.

Compassion can never coexist with judgment because judgment creates the distance, the distinction, which prevents us from really being with the other.

The older brother (of the prodigal) isn't the only one who can't stand the father's demonstration of compassion.

Billy Graham: "I said one word – forgiveness – and I got all kinds of ugly letters about that...."

Compassion has nothing to do with not holding people accountable for their actions or letting dangerous behavior go unchecked.

Did everyone respond to Jesus' compassion with a change of heart, mind, and direction?

Chapter 9: Why Did Jesus Eat With Sinners?

MODERN OBSERVATIONS:

Do we provide a non-judgmental environment for others to reveal themselves to us?[1]

There is a popular adage, "What would Jesus do?" The question should be "What *did* Jesus do?"[2]

Before you scrawl a Bible verse on a sign and wave it in someone's face, I would ask you to take that someone to dinner....Yeah, I know it's easier to stand on a parade route with your friends being obnoxious and self-righteous, but, in case you haven't noticed, that doesn't work. The only thing strident arrogance is good for is hardening hearts, fostering resentment, and creating animosity.[3]

Identify with what I understand to be Jesus' fundamental purpose: to reconcile humans to God and one another.[4]

No one knows the limits of God's grace.[5]

The conflict between exclusion and embrace was at the very heart of the conflict between Jesus and the religious establishment of his day.[6]

THE BIBLICAL TEXT: Matthew 9:9-13:

> *As Jesus was walking along, he saw a man called Matthew sitting at the tax booth; and he said to him, "Follow me." And he got up and followed him. And as he sat at dinner in the house, many tax collectors and sinners came and were sitting with him and his disciples. When the Pharisees saw this, they said to his disciples, "Why does your teacher eat with tax collectors and sinners?" But when he heard this he said, "Those who are well have no need of a physician, but those who are sick. Go and learn what this means, 'I desire mercy, not sacrifice.' For I have come to call not the righteous but sinners.*

Creating Trouble

When I read the above text, I come to only one shocking conclusion: Jesus is going out of his way to be a troublemaker. Why else would he do such a thing? Jesus' fame as a teacher and healer is spreading like wildfire. No one has heard or seen anything like Jesus before. His popularity among the people is soaring. And then he makes this misstep. He makes this strategic error. Just a little later in Matthew's Gospel (11:19) Jesus tells us what his enemies are saying about him: *Look, a glutton and a drunkard, a friend of tax collectors and sinners.* This should come as no surprise. In this one episode, he gives them plenty of ammunition for both charges.

As he passes a custom's booth set up to collect import and export taxes, Jesus asks the man seated there to become his disciple. (This is not the first time Matthew has seen Jesus.) I can only imagine the open-mouthed horror of the other disciples as Matthew stands and says, "Sign me up." Tax collectors were on the short list of "scum." They were universally hated and were banned from the synagogue. And, no doubt, rightly so. (In addition: their money was not accepted as alms and their evidence was not accepted in the law court.) They were part of a tax system that had abuse written all over it. The Romans auctioned off the right to collect certain taxes. The highest bidder got the contract with the right to keep as his commission all he collected above the bid. There was no set amount for most taxes and that meant nobody knew exactly what they owed. They owed as much as the tax collector could collect.

Most tax collectors got wealthy. Although probably in the employ of Herod Antipas and not directly in the service of Rome, Matthew was still numbered among the hated and wealthy tax collectors. His wealth is indicated by the lavish banquet he throws to which he invites his friends, Jesus, and Jesus' disciples. (We learn whose house it is from Luke 5:27-32). His friends come. Jesus and his disciples come.

Jesus deliberately antagonizes every clear thinking lover of God's commandments by asking a tax collector to be his disciple and then by joining in table fellowship with a group no respectable religious person would ever be seen with, much less eat with. (The dinner was probably held in a large courtyard in easy view of those who passed by.) The big question: Why did Jesus eat with sinners?

Earl Warren, while Governor of California, once opened his address to a political gathering with: "I'm pleased to see such a dense crowd here tonight." A voice shouted, "Don't be so pleased, Governor, we ain't all that dense." The crowd at Matthew's house was not a dense crowd. They would not have attended if they had not wanted to. There must have been something about Jesus to make him attractive to the kind of crowd gathered there: wealthy, sophisticated, worldly, not excessively religious – not picky in their religion.

> The Gospel writers faithfully noted the words of Jesus, but they did not record in writing things like the twinkle in the eye, the gentle smile, the grin, the hearty laugh, the tone and inflection of voice, the hand gestures.[7]

It always amazes me how at home Jesus felt with the people known as sinners and how at home they felt with him – and how much out of place he felt with the religious leaders of his day and how out of place they felt with him.

The Need for the List of Sinners

I can think of at least one reason the Pharisees keep harping on Jesus' association with tax collectors and sinners. And why good religious folk still need such categories.

A good many years ago, *The New York Times* reported that Richard Harbert spotted an apparently homeless man sitting atop a shopping cart loaded with an array of plastic bags and other belongings. The man wasn't the usual panhandler. There was no cup in sight; he simply held up a brown corrugated cardboard sign that read "TELL ME OFF FOR $2." Mr. Harbert said he was tempted for a moment, but he was in too good a mood to take advantage of the offer.

Well, that might be the best $2 you ever spend! Where else can you tell off somebody with no repercussions? Where else can you get the chance to feel taller and superior to one who is definitely your financial, moral, ethical, and spiritual inferior? Would he be sitting atop that stolen shopping cart if he weren't? Don't we all need lesser persons to point out the contrast of our greater stature? Don't all of us truly good people need to keep our designated list of sinners so that by contrast others can see how good we truly are?

That seems to have been the name of the game in Jesus' day. Do you remember the story he tells about two men who go to the Temple to pray? (Luke 18:9-14). I suspect it was something Jesus had actually seen and heard. One of the two men (a tax collector) stands apart from everyone else with his head down, uttering a single, repeated line: *"God, be merciful to me a sinner."* (Looking up was the usual stance in prayer.) The other character in the story is a Pharisee who announces: *"God, I thank you that I am not like other people: thieves, rogues, adulterers, or even like this tax collector."* He was into comparative religion big time.

If you choose the right crowd, you can always look good by comparison. But looking good by looking down on others is never something Jesus endorses. In fact, if you know the end of the story, you remember it is the tax collector who goes home right with God, the Pharisee just goes home. Biblical righteousness is not something you get by contrast. Goodness is not achieved by drawing a circle, labeling it "sinners," and placing oneself on the outside of the circle.

It was probably Thomas Aquinas who carried this to its logical extreme: "In order that nothing be wanting to the happiness of the blessed in Heaven, a perfect view is granted them of the tortures of the damned." Jonathan Edwards added his twist by saying that "the view of the misery of (those in Hell) will double the ardor of the love and gratitude of the saints in heaven." I guess they believed you could tell off these people eternally and it wouldn't even cost you $2!

A Lack of Biblical Knowledge

Jesus hears the question of the Pharisees and tells his critics that if they knew their Bible better they would know what he is doing. He says this to the group that thinks they know the Scriptures better than anyone else. Jesus quotes from Hosea 6:6 where God proclaims: *"I desire mercy, not sacrifice."* What really must gall them is when Jesus tells these self-proclaimed Scripture experts: "*Go and learn what this means.*"

> In 1989, Mother Teresa visited Phoenix to open a home for the destitute. During that brief visit, she was interviewed by KTAR, the largest radio station there. In a private moment the announcer asked Mother Teresa if there was anything he could do for her. He was expecting her to request a contribution or media-help to raise money for her new home for the impoverished in Phoenix. Instead, she replied, "Yes, there is. Find somebody nobody else loves and love them."[8]

As he sits in Matthew's house, Jesus is with some of the people who most need him. Unfortunately, they are sinners. But, of course, that is Jesus' point when he tells the Pharisees, *"Those who are well have no need of a physician, but those who are sick."* By quoting Hosea 6:6, I don't believe Jesus was issuing a blanket condemnation of the sacrificial system or that he totally ignored the righteousness that was exhibited in the lives of the Pharisees. I believe he is insisting that mercy become priority one in God's book of religion; he maintains that excluding and despising other people is not the door to effective evangelism.

The Pharisees think Jesus is with the wrong crowd. Jesus says he is with the right crowd. Mercy and grace make the Pharisees nervous. Jesus takes them as the primary attributes and gifts of his Father.

If you were never able to hear William Augustus Jones, you missed someone extremely gifted and extraordinary. Years ago, I was privileged to hear him at the Stetson Pastor's School. He crafted one of the most fascinating sermon titles I have ever heard. He titled his sermon "Jesus, the Junk Man." Among the things he said: "The God I serve doesn't throw anybody away. God is in the restoration and reclamation business....Jesus is a junk man. He goes around and picks up scraps of humanity and puts them together for something glorious....It is our job to set up shop as close to the gates of Hell as possible and send traffic in the other direction." My comment: God IS in the restoration and reclamation business! Jesus is looking for junked human beings who are ready to be put together for something glorious!

Many have heard the story that comes from the 15th century about the Florentine sculptor Agostino d'Antonio who discarded a huge block of marble after failed attempts to produce a spectacular sculpture. The block of marble was badly disfigured and lay idle for forty years. Then another sculptor took an interest in it. He saw beyond the ugly block of marble to something he felt he could achieve. He began work and his finished creation is on display in Florence today. Yes, the sculptor is Michelangelo and the result is the celebrated "David."

All it took was the touch of a master's hand. The touch of the Master's hand still works the miracle of reshaping and reclaiming and making something astounding out of the discarded, the tossed aside, the written off.

We don't know what happened to the crowd of sinners who ate with Jesus that day in Matthew's house. We do know that Matthew becomes one of the twelve. And even if he did not author the Gospel, it is absolutely astounding that this despised tax collector, this piece of junk marble, has his name attached to one of the four Gospels, to the very first book in the New Testament. Just goes to show what Jesus can do with a sinner.

Of course, that's why Jesus eats with sinners. Those who sat down with Jesus that day in Matthew's house were never the same again. You never know what will happen when you sit down at the table with Jesus the junk man.

[1]Matthew Kelly, *The Rhythm of Life* (New York, Simon & Schuster, 2004), 56.

[2]Carlton Pearson, *The Gospel of Inclusion* (New York, Simon & Schuster, 2006), 74.

[3]Dan Merchant, *Lord, Save Us From Your Followers* (Nashville, Thomas Nelson, 2008), 182.

[4]David Awbrey, *Finding Hope in the Age of Melancholy* (Boston, Little, Brown, 1999), 220

[5]Ibid., 221.

[6]Manfred Brauch, *Abusing Scripture* (Downers Grove, Il., InterVarsity Press, 2009), 239.

[7]Cal Samra, *The Joyful Christ* (San Francisco, Harper & Row, 1985), 7.

[8]*Homiletics Magazine,* Winter, '98, 79.

Why Did Jesus Eat With Sinners?
Points to Ponder

Do we provide a non-judgmental environment for others to reveal themselves to us?

Jesus deliberately antagonizes every clear thinking lover of God's commandments by asking a tax collector to be his disciple and then by joining in table fellowship with a group no respectable religious person would ever be seen with, much less eat with.

It always amazes me how at home Jesus felt with the people known as sinners and how at home they felt with him.

Don't all of us truly good people need to keep our designated list of sinners so that by contrast others can see how good we truly are?

Jesus maintains that excluding and despising other people is not the door to effective evangelism.

William Augustus Jones: "The God I serve doesn't throw anybody away. God is in the restoration and reclamation business...Jesus is the junk man."

Even if he did not author the Gospel, it is absolutely astounding that this despised tax collector, this piece of junk marble, has his name attached to one of the four Gospels, to the very first book in the New Testament.

You never know what will happen when you sit down at the table with Jesus the junk man.

Reflections on Part III: "In the Meantime" Priorities

Being misunderstood comes with the territory of preaching. I continue to be amazed at the things people tell me they heard in a sermon. Some of their quotes are things I know I never said. But they are not telling me what I said, they are telling me what they heard. That is one of the reasons I have always enjoyed Bible studies and workshops so much - they provide the setting for dialogue and the clarification of things so easily misunderstood. I have also discovered that putting things in print is no guarantee of the reception of your intended meaning.

My preaching has always emphasized what I believe to be the emphasis we find in the Gospels. The problem with sermons or subjects in a book is that you cannot possibly say everything that needs to be said about any subject. You cannot possibly include all the subtleties and "on the other hand" situations that could be cited. That is why I really prefer dialogue situations. I not only need to have time to clarify what I am trying to say but I also need to know what others have heard me saying and where they find difficulties or disagreements with what I am saying. (More about this in Chapter 11.)

If there are genuine priorities for living in difficult times, they are my willingness to assume full responsibility for my decisions and actions and my stance of compassion and openness to the world around me. *God so loved the world* (John 3:16) is probably the best known verse in the Bible. In four shocking words it gives God's stance toward the world he knows beyond any human understanding. He did not send his Son into the world *to condemn the world* (John 3:17) - another remarkable stance. When we are told not to love the world (I John 2:15), this refers to the philosophy and ways of the world that are divorced from the God of creation and redemption. We are not told to hate the people of the world.

Some will find it strange that when Karen Armstrong

received the TED award in 2007 with $100,000, she asked this private organization "to help her create, launch, and propagate a Charter for Compassion that would be written by leading thinkers from a variety of major faiths and would restore compassion to the heart of religious and moral life."[1] The charter was launched on November 12, 2009; her book details the charter and a recommended twelve steps.

In her book, *Twelve Steps to a Compassionate Life,* Armstrong goes all the way back to creation to make her case for compassion:

> In their interpretation of the biblical doctrine of creation, the rabbis focused on the fact that all human beings were made in God's image. To show disrespect to anyone was therefore regarded as a denial of God himself and tantamount to atheism, and murder was not simply a crime against humanity but a sacrilege.[2]

Regardless of the apparent distortions, the Bible plainly states that the great gift of creation was the making of human beings in God's own image. There is not a single passage anywhere in Scripture that indicates this does not hold true for certain groups. To recognize all people as created in God's image is the first step on the road to compassion.

In a cartoon, an older man is sitting across the desk from a person who asks him, "Do you prefer to be called 'Geriatric,' 'Elderly' or 'Senior'?" With a heavy frown, the man responds "I prefer to be called Mr. Stevens." Unpacking that cartoon would require another book! One of my early discoveries in visiting nursing homes was how much those who were there needed to be called by their names. Not role titles - Mom, Pop, Grandma, Grandpa, etc. - but by the names that signify they are persons created in the image of God before they are anything else. That is another reason why in funeral homilies I am very careful to use full names – both married and maiden, and - perhaps most importantly - first names.

I think Lyndon Johnson spoke for all of us in this observation:

> When Lyndon Johnson announced that he was leaving Washington and returning to his ranch in Texas to live, some asked in disbelief, "Why? Why are you leaving the excitement of Washington to return out there?" "Because," Johnson said, "Out there they ask about you when you are sick, and they cry when you die."[3]

[1]Karen Armstrong, *Twelve Steps To a Compassionate Life* (New York, Alfred A. Knopf, 2010), 6.

[2]Ibid., 53.

[3]Douglas Weaver, *From Our Christian Heritage* (Macon, Smyth & Helwys, 1997), #1608B.

Part IV: Discovering Unique Opportunities

Chapter 10: Finding the Growing Edge

MODERN OBSERVATIONS:

My father used to say that if he ever wrote a self-help book, he would call it: *Overcoming Peace of Mind.*[1]

The first lesson for enduring happiness is this: Celebrate your progress.... The second lesson for enduring happiness is: Just do the next right thing.[2]

With the right attitude, even scrubbing floors can make us grow.[3]

Change occurs at the edge of complexity.[4]

The ways in which we need to grow are usually those we are the most supremely defended against and are least willing to admit even exist, let alone take an undefended, mindful peek at and then act on to change.[5]

Doing theology...entails for us...the acquisition of a critical self-awareness which may well produce in us acute forms of mental discomfort.[6]

As I struggled with whether to embrace this experience or banish it, a friend said to me, "If you think God leads you only beside still waters, think again. God will also lead you beside turbulent waters. If you have the courage to enter, you'll think you're drowning. But actually you're being churned into something new. It's okay, Sue, dive in."[7]

THE BIBLICAL TEXTS: John 16:12-13; Romans 5:1-5:

"I still have many things to say to you, but you cannot bear them now. When the Spirit of truth comes, he will guide you into all truth...."
Therefore, since we are justified by faith, we have peace with God through our Lord Jesus Christ, through whom we have obtained access to this grace in which we stand, and we boast in our hope of sharing the glory of God. And not only that, but we also boast in our sufferings, knowing that suffering produces endurance, and endurance produces character, and character produces hope, and hope does not disappoint us, because God's love has been poured into our hearts through the Holy Spirit that has been given to us.

Healthy Spirituality

Often books seem to literally jump off the shelf. One of those experiences occurred while I was browsing in a bookstore (an addiction!) and picked up a book by an author unknown to me. It was the title that grabbed me: *And Grace Will Lead Me Home.* The subtitle of the book is: *A Spiritual Journey.* Authored by John Powers, it is an allegory similar to Bunyan's *Pilgrim's Progress.* I give you only two thoughts for our time:

> There is...no religion worthy of faith, that can take away the pain of life. Religion for security and safety's sake is mere idolatry. Religion is useless without a spirituality that helps you live positively with pain and suffering.[8]

> Healthy spirituality begins with this insight. We humans are incomplete, unfinished and imperfect....We suffer because we attempt to deny our unfinishedness, strive to avoid all pain, and fight to subdue God and the creative universe. The primary task of spirituality is to teach us to make home and soul out of the necessary freedom and inevitable pains of life.[9]

These disturbing words echo Paul's reason for "boasting" in our Romans text. We recall this is the Paul whom we find with his coworker Silas at midnight in a dark prison cell singing hymns of praise to God. Are there lessons in darkness, trouble, difficulty, and suffering that can be learned nowhere else? Unfortunately, the answer to that question is a thunderous "Yes!"

I discovered ten rules for dieting that I believe everyone will be glad to hear. A few will indicate the tone of the remaining ones:

> If you eat something and no one else sees it, it has no calories.

> If you drink a diet drink with a candy bar, the calories in the candy bar are canceled out by the diet drink.
>
> When you eat with someone else, the calories don't count if you don't eat more than they do.
>
> Things licked off knives and spoons have no calories, provided you are in the process of preparing something. Examples are peanut butter on a knife while making a peanut butter and jelly sandwich and ice cream on a spoon when making a sundae.
>
> Movie related foods do not have additional calories because they are part of the entire entertainment package and not part of one's personal fuel, including Milk Duds, buttered popcorn, Hershey Bars, Junior Mints, Red Hots, and Tootsie Rolls.
>
> Cookie pieces contain no calories. The process of breaking causes calorie drainage.[10]

We read a list like this and lament, "Oh, if only it were so!" We know it isn't. We also know there isn't an "easy" list for most things in life. One author of a self-help book has for his opening sentence: "Most worthwhile things in life are a lot of trouble." If this is not bad enough, our faith takes one step further. It is in that trouble that you can really learn the most. And I mean real trouble and things we really need to learn.

Perhaps the most quoted line from C. S. Lewis is: "God whispers to us in our pleasures, speaks in our conscience, but shouts in our pains; it is his megaphone to rouse a deaf world."

Most are shocked to discover that this learning through suffering has no exceptions – including Jesus. Hebrews 5:7-10:

> *Although he was Son, he learned obedience through what he suffered; and having been made perfect, he became the source of eternal salvation for all who obey him, having been designated by God a high priest according to the order of Melchizedek.*

"Jesus' sonship did not immunize him from the necessity of learning as every genuinely human being must learn."[11] If anyone could have escaped this process of learning it would have been Jesus. But then, if he had, he would not have been fully human. He could not have understood us. We would not have a high priest before whom we can come with boldness, knowing we are fully understood. That is why the author of Hebrews can label it *the throne of grace* and assure us we will *receive mercy and find grace to help in time of need* (Hebrews 4:16). Some of the worst experiences of my life have come when I attempted to "confess" before someone who had no idea how anyone could be so imperfect!

From the Depths

You would think that when Paul writes, *Therefore, since we are justified by faith, we have peace with God through our Lord Jesus Christ, through whom we have obtained access to this grace in which we now stand,* that everything following would be joy and light. Not so! Immediately following this shout of praise, he continues with: *we also boast in our sufferings.* The Greek word used is literally *pressure* and can also be translated: *troubles, hardships.* He boasts because some of the greatest things in life happen to us and in us: *endurance, character, and hope.* That is, of course, only if....

A young boy was listening to a sermon on the book of Job. In the midst of hearing all the disasters that Job endured, he turned to his father and asked, "Why doesn't he sue somebody?" This is the temptation. Or simply to be crushed by trouble and suffering. Job's wife counseled him to curse God and die. That's always an option. Or to rush through the suffering. Or to sedate it. But Job would have missed the greatest lessons of his life. He would have missed becoming all that he was meant to become.

Endurance, character, hope and a lot of other things can be learned only if we see them as part of the growing edge of trouble, only if we are ready to let God use that suffering, only if we believe that God's goal for us is not comfort but character, only if we believe that God has a great purpose for each of us, only if we believe God wants us to really BE somebody.

1. Endurance: learning how to keep on keeping on, to never give up, to even, as Moffatt translates it, *triumph in our troubles.*

2. Character: the Greek word for metal that has passed through the fire so that everything base has been purged out of it.

3. Hope: the solid conviction that the love of God supports our lives.

Where else, except in trouble, can you learn the truth of Psalm 46?

> *God is our refuge and strength, an ever-present help in trouble. Therefore we will not fear, though the earth give way and the mountains fall into the heart of the sea, though its waters roar and foam and the mountains quake with their surging (New International Version).*

You don't learn that until everything else is gone and you have no other refuge. Paul and Silas knew the truth of this psalm in a prison cell. We are most inspired by those whose lives are filled with trouble and yet marked by endurance, character, and hope. To see in every situation an opportunity for growth of some sort is to live a life trusting that God's providence is always operative. The book of Lamentations is hardly ever read and rarely used as the basis for a sermon. Who wants to read this litany of doom and gloom after the fall of Jerusalem and the unthinkable destruction of everything that constituted life for the chosen people? Yet, tucked in this litany of sorrow, we find these words:

> The steadfast love of the Lord never ceases,
> his mercies never come to an end;
> they are new every morning;
> great is your faithfulness.
> (Lamentations 3:22)

From the most mournful of all the biblical writings comes the basis for the hymn "Great Is Thy Faithfulness."

Living on the Edge

I remember one writer who urges all of us to use "horse sense" in our desire to grow and discover. Just like a horse that begins to graze where it is, moving from one clump of grass to another. Taking the next step to the next area of nourishment is the "grazing principle" he maintains was at the root of all great discoveries. We can see only the edge of things anyway. We can only live on the edges. Thomas Carlyle: "Our main business is not to see what lies at a distance but to do what lies clearly at hand." The question, IN EVERY SITUATION, is: "What is obvious to me right now?" Or as Matthew Kelly prescribes as one of the rules for happiness: Do the next right thing.

In a few simple words, one writer (Stanley Mooneyham) gives a twist on this insight: "As Henri Nouwen, my currently favorite author says...." What a great phrase: "my currently favorite author." He found someone who is speaking to him where he is now. His currently favorite author will change. That's okay. What is important is to be aware of what it is that can speak to you most clearly where you are. The Bible uses two words for time: *chronos* and *kairos. Chronos* is measured time – hours, days, weeks, etc. *Kairos* is used in phrases like *in the fullness of time.* Teachable moments come to us. They come in the form of a special author, friend, event, etc. It is the moment of *kairos* in our lives.

To believe that in every situation we can find a *kairos* moment means that nothing that comes our way will be wasted. I cannot even imagine how the exiles in Babylon felt. The deportation to a strange land and culture in the wake of the destruction of their beloved city and Temple was bad enough. But to be taunted by those who worshipped another god must have been unbearable; the common belief was that the god who triumphed was the true god. In the eyes of the Babylonians, the God of Israel had been defeated. So how could they sing the songs of Zion in a strange land while their jeering captors made up the audience? Finding the growing edge in this, another wilderness experience, was no easy matter.

Perhaps too often we look for a major or significant opportunity instead of remembering that Jesus tells his disciples he is going to parcel out a little bit of spiritual truth at a time. And the promised Holy Spirit would *escort* them into all the truth. The Greek word *guide* means *escort.* The Spirit is our escort. Escorting us into truth the same way Jesus led his disciples into truth. My paraphrase of John 16:12-13: Jesus said, "I have much more to say to you but you can't handle it all now, so I'll let the Holy Spirit give it to you in small doses so that you will not be overwhelmed." John Powell has written that profound change is a wide, round curve that can be negotiated only slowly, not a sharp corner that can be turned all at once.[12]

I always add a note that recalls bygone days. In Jesus' classroom there are no hickory sticks or dunce caps. No one has to stand in the corner or have their knuckles rapped. Only the words: "Let's try again. Here, I'll help you." We'll never have to worry about getting "the stupid award" (one for which I have qualified on more than one occasion!). We will never have to worry about being shamed for where we are or for what we don't know or even for how we happen to be feeling at the moment. (A needed prescription for some churches I have known.) Truth, truth about myself and my life and my relationship with others and with God is not easy to handle. But there is always a growing edge where I can begin.

I once served a church in a comfortably large city. On one of my visits to a homebound member I was impressed by her ability to be alive and productive in her very restricted situation. She scanned the local newspaper for stories of achievement on the part of community residents. She clipped those articles, wrote a brief note of congratulations, and mailed both, often to persons she had never met. She told me she was in the ministry of affirmation and encouragement. You can hardly imagine the response that came from those she affirmed and encouraged. She was the happiest homebound member I have ever visited! In her Babylon, in her prison cell, she had discovered how to sing the Lord's song. And all who heard it were truly blessed.

It's About How We Live

I've saved the most disturbing aspect of this chapter until last. Spiritual growth is always about how I am doing in relationship to others. The so-called "spiritual-disciplines" are things that enable me to live better (more redemptively) in the world right now. "Just do the next right thing" (Matthew Kelly) may well be the best clue to finding the growing edge in our lives. When we pray *Thy kingdom come, thy will be DONE on earth as it is in heaven,* the emphasis (as I have indicated) is all about something we are to be doing. To live as Kingdom citizens (Matthew 5-7) means that our lives will be characterized by a certain kind of behavior.

Even in difficult times, there is always a growing edge.

In his 1946 book *Man's Search for Meaning,* Holocaust

survivor Victor Frankl gave the definitive rebuttal to the belief that we are nothing beyond creatures of our environment. He observed concentration camp inmates living in barbaric conditions and emerged with evidence that fate was an illusion. "We who lived in concentration camps can remember the men who walked through the huts comforting others, giving away their last piece of bread. They may have been few in number, but they offer sufficient proof that everything that can be taken from a man but one thing: the last of the human freedoms – to choose one's attitude in any given set of circumstances, to choose one's own way."[13]

Rabbi Shmuley provides this reminder: Judaism...proclaimed that what people make of their lives depends entirely on their actions."[14] This is exactly what Jesus says in Matthew 7:16: *You will know them by their fruits.* It is the emphasis of Paul in Galatians 5:22: *...the fruit of the Spirit is love, joy, peace, patience, kindness, generosity, faithfulness, gentleness, and self-control.* The heavy emphasis on our relationships is underscored in verses 25-26: *If we live by the Spirit, let us be guided by the Spirit. Let us not become conceited, competing with one another, envying one another.* The kind of truth into which the Spirit escorts us is primarily truth about our relationships with others.

Jesus' present day disciples are still arguing about who is the greatest (Mark 9:34), finding specks in the eyes of other believers (Matthew 7:3), questioning those who are not exactly their kind of Christian (Mark 9:38), wanting to call down fiery judgment instead of showers of blessing (Luke 9:54), and failing to acknowledge that the way they love one another is the number one indicator that they are a part of the Jesus' Way (John 13:35). ("Followers of the Way" is probably the first label applied to Christians. Perhaps it ought to be resurrected.)

To reduce the Great Commission (Matthew 28:19-20) to "getting people saved" is like encouraging people to attend a Broadway show and leave after the overture. Salvation is all about the curtain going up on a new life. Most people who reject the Christian faith have little problem with Jesus; they have many problems with those who claim to represent him. The reason *Lord, Save Us From Your Followers* created such an uproar is that it raised some very disturbing questions. (More about this book in Chapter 11.) It asks the question "What did Jesus do?" instead of "What would Jesus do?" His teachings and actions were a seamless whole. He loved the unlovable, he touched the untouchable, he included the outcasts, he welcomed the unfit, and he demonstrated an inclusive gospel that tore down every boundary. We are saved to do just what he did.

Have I found this difficult? Absolutely! My growing edge I frequently found to be the last thing I would have chosen. In one pastorate, a few months after my arrival, a deacon informed me that one person had been waiting for the new minister to come before she presented herself for membership. Not unusual, except that this person was African-American and the church was all white. No other church in the town had a "mixed" congregation. I need to tell you a story you will hardly believe; it is the story as I remember it.

In the next deacons' meeting the matter came up for discussion. One man spoke up, "I hear she's being paid $40 a week to attend here." My response: "Oh, I wouldn't let that out if I were you. A lot of people might want to get in on that." He looked at me in stunned silence. It was decided that a senior deacon (who was a true saint) and I were to make a visit to the inquirer and bring back a report. We made our call and at the next deacons' meeting informed the group that we saw no reason why Ms. ______ should not be received as a member. Now it was just a waiting game.

The next few Sundays were not easy ones for me. This was a time of high national anxiety over racial issues and there were few calm voices to be heard. One Sunday I awoke with mild flu-like symptoms but decided I had to be in the service. That was one Sunday when, before announcing the "invitation hymn," I silently prayed that no one would come! I didn't know if I was up to handling the situation. However, on the first stanza, Ms._____ came forward. Three women to my right put their hands over their hearts and fell back in the pew. I felt certain this would be my last Sunday as pastor.

On the next stanza, a couple with two young children came forward to join. I had never seen them before. On the third stanza, a young couple came forward to join. I had never seen them before. On the final stanza, a family of five came forward to join. I had never seen them before. When I motioned for the congregation to be seated, most of them were in a state of shock - not over the first person who came but over the record number of persons who were presenting themselves for membership.

I began by presenting Ms.___for membership and asking all those who welcomed her to make it known by the uplifted hand. (I never ask for any opposition.) As I moved to the first family that had come, a member rose from a pew in the back and called out, "I rise to a point of order. I move that the matter of Ms.______ asking for membership be discussed in a business meeting." I paused for a moment and innocently inquired, "I'm not sure I understand. We have received her as we receive all members." He said a couple of more words I couldn't quite make out and then our chairman of deacons, seated on the third row, unwound his tall frame (he always reminded me of Gregory Peck in *To Kill a Mockingbird)* and said quietly, "I'm sorry, Mr._____, but I'm going to have to rule you out of order and ask you to be seated."

The end of the story is that the only family to leave the church was the family of the deacon who tried to circulate the rumor of $40 a week. A sidebar is that the choir had made a decision I didn't learn about until later. If things had gotten out of control, they were prepared to begin singing, "Jesus loves the little children, all the children of the world. Red and yellow black and white, they are precious in his sight. Jesus loves the little children of the world." And they were not going to stop singing!

When we find the growing edge (or have it chosen for

us!), we are not left on our own. The promised Spirit will be there. I never did ask why all those people decided to present themselves for membership before I ever talked with them. (That was not a requirement.) I had not asked the chairman of deacons to intervene if something erupted when Ms._____ came forward. I do not doubt for one moment the movement of the Spirit in the service that morning. Truly, he was our escort.

It's Right Here, Right Now

As a conclusion to this chapter, I give a series of quotes from *Wherever You Go There You Are* by Jon Kabat-Zinn:

1. Like it or not, this moment is all we really have to work with.
2. In every moment, we find ourselves at the crossroad of here and now.
3. To find our way, we will need to pay more attention to this moment. It is the only time that we have in which to live, grow, feel, and change.
4. What happens now, in this moment, influences what happens next.
5. Our lives unfold only in moments.
6. The habit of ignoring our present moments in favor of others yet to come leads directly to a pervasive lack of awareness of the web of life in which we are embedded.[15]

[1]Kathleen Norris, *Acadia & Me,* 15.

[2]Matthew Kelly, *Perfectly Yourself,* 26, 53.

[3]Monks of New Skete, *In the Spirit of Happiness* (Boston, Little,Brown, and Company, 1999), 281.

[4]Bob Sitz, *Not Trying Too Hard* (Washington, Alban Institute, 2001), 237.

[5]Jan Kabat-Zinn, *Wherever You Go There You Are* (New York, Hyperion, 1994), 76.

[6]Douglas Hall, *Thinking the Faith,* 19.

[7]Sue Monk Kidd, *When the Heart Waits,* 10.

[8]John Powers, *And Grace Will Lead Me Home* (New York, McCracken Press, 1994), 32.

[9]Ibid., 32, 34.

[10]*Homiletics Magazine,* 8/97, 31.

[11]*The Broadman Bible Commentary,* XII, 42.

[12]John Powell, *The Secret of Staying in Love* (Niles, Il., Argus Communications, 1974), 44.

[13]Samuel Boteach, *Renewal* (New York, Basic Books, 2010), 5.

[14]Ibid., p. 3.

[15]Jon Kabat-Zinn, *Wherever You Go There You Are,* xiii, xv, xvi, 4, 5.

Finding the Growing Edge
Points to Ponder

Are there lessons in darkness, trouble, difficulty, and suffering that can be learned nowhere else?

There isn't an "easy" list for most things in life.

Some of the worst experiences of my life have come when I attempted to "confess" before someone who had no idea how anyone could be so imperfect.

Endurance, character, hope, and a lot of other things can be learned only if we see them as a part of the growing edge of trouble.

To see in every situation an opportunity for growth of some sort is to live a life trusting that God's providence is always operative.

The question in every situation is: "What is obvious to me right now?"

Jesus tells his disciples that he is going to parcel out a little bit of spiritual truth at a time.

There is always a growing edge where I can begin.

The growing edge is often the place of the Spirit's most profound work.

Chapter 11: The Time for Conversation and Dialogue

MODERN OBSERVATIONS:

When judgment and renunciation replace empathy and pluralism, democratic culture cannot survive; conversations end, and the ongoing process of democratic argumentation is snipped off....[1]

Our communication model is broken. In this consumer culture we've been trained to accept ad slogans, labels, sound bites, and bumper-sticker slogans as adequate. These micro-blips of information reduce the complexity of an issue, strip essential meaning from it and ultimately snuff out conversation.[2]

Rely on conversation as your primary medium for information spreading. It builds relationships, communicates emotion as well as information, establishes trustworthiness, and is relatively low-cost.[3]

Dialogue, I shall suggest, is not merely a strategy, but it is a practice that is congruent with our deepest nature, made as we are in the image of a dialogic God.[4]

"Argument is born of having the answer; conversation is born of having a question." Robert Cornwall.

A gracious church is a safe place to ask questions, explore new ideas, admit our struggles, and seek assistance. Sadly, this is not the nature of most congregations. Too often, a church is where people who already agree gather to have their viewpoints reinforced.[5]

A gracious church is a place where people can come with questions, doubts, and struggles without fear of being condemned. Our focus is not on supplying quick and easy answers to difficult problems, but creating the space to think and explore.[6]

THE BIBLICAL TEXT: Acts 15:12, 22, 28-29 (New Living Translation):

> *There was no further discussion, and everyone listened as Barnabas and Paul told about the miraculous signs and wonders God had done through them among the Gentiles.*
> *Then the apostles and elders and the whole church in Jerusalem chose delegates and they sent them to Antioch of Syria with Paul and Barnabas to report their decision.*
> *"For it has seemed good to the Holy Spirit and us to lay no greater burden on you than these requirements: You must abstain from eating food offered to idols, from consuming or eating the meat of strangled animals, and from sexual immorality. If you do this, you will do well...."*

In Search of a Model

My wife and I have lived in the same community for over thirty years. We can't think of living anywhere else; we couldn't ask for better or more helpful neighbors. However, about a year ago we were out of town when a "discussion" was scheduled at a city council meeting. Many felt the deer population was getting out of control. (Only last night we saw eight deer two doors from us in a neighbor's front yard.) The discussion was circumvented by a podium-pounding, tearful voice that threatened legal action if her wishes were not honored. The committee that was supposed to bring back a recommendation was never called back and the issue remains off the table.

Unfortunately, this appears to be the prevalent model for the discussion of almost any issue. There is no attempt at anything resembling real dialogue. Some issues are so hot that when I'm asked how I would lead a group in tackling them, my only suggestion is that we line up the opposing sides opposite each other and, on command, just begin throwing things at one another. In the shocked silence that follows, I whisper, "That's really all we are doing anyway." Far too much of what we see are shouting matches, name calling (labeling), character assassination, and truth distortion and misrepresentation with the only goal to win at whatever the cost (that cost usually paid by the larger community).

As I write this (January 2012), we are in the midst of a political campaign that has several months to go. I told my wife I believed the best way to handle the rhetoric on all sides was to move to Australia until it was over. She has not begun packing. My personal discouragement about even a modest attempt at what we used to call conversation and dialogue is not even entertained. The only purpose seems to be to portray your opponent in the worst way possible and portray your idea as the only one any sensible person can accept. Plus – paint a picture of disaster if your way is not endorsed. There is no attempt to listen to opposing points of view.

The comment did not come to me first hand but a friend vouches for its authenticity. A prominent denominational leader was asked how he intended to dialogue with those who had different opinions. His exact words: "Dialogue? If you have the truth, what is there to dialogue about?" Risking a too heavy rejoinder, my only comment was: "This seems to have been the approach the scribes and Pharisees took with Jesus!" If this is your stance, then those who don't agree with you are in error, they are guilty of false doctrine, they are instruments of the demonic. They are evil. Neither they nor their ideas can be tolerated. *Come out from them, and be separate from them* (2 Corinthians 6:17) becomes the mantra.

Most of the debating I hear only contributes to further polarization. If you have all the truth on an issue (ignoring Paul's confession that *now, we see in a mirror, dimly* - I Corinthians 13:12), then you simply put on your armor and fight the "good" fight. This is not to say that we should not have convictions or beliefs; I do not believe that life or faith can be devoid of these. As I have gotten older, my list of "absolute essentials" in the faith is smaller than it used to be. The paradox is that I don't think I believe less, I think I believe more! In other chapters and other books I have issued the challenge to major on the biblical essentials, what I call the biblical mountaintops. The recent "worship wars" are simply another among the many battles over things that should not be the determining factors in our willingness to fellowship (*kononia)* with one another.

Living in difficult times calls for conversation and dialogue – not shouting matches. It's bad enough when what can only be called "hate speech" comes from the political arena; it is unthinkable when it comes from the religious community. When did we lose sight of the ONE thing Jesus said would mark us for the world out as his followers? *By this everyone will know that you are my disciples, if you have love for one another* (John 13:35). This follows what can be called Jesus' Eleventh Commandment: *I give you a new commandment, that you love one another. Just as I have loved you, you also should love one another* (John 13:34). This is the new Moses standing on the highest of the biblical mountaintops. There are many passages that puzzle me; I understand this one all too well.

A Two-Thousand Year Old Model

Our text from Acts 15 tells us how the church resolved its first major conflict. Since there are few good current models, we will go back 2,000 years to see how successful conflict resolution works. The church conference in Acts 15 has a positive outcome. In every church I served, we always had a difficult time getting a good crowd for a business meeting. I am like Frank, age 13, who is quoted in the book *Wit and Wisdom of the Peanut Butter Gang:* "Riding your bike on ice is not as exciting as planning it."[7] Talking about the democratic process in the church and meeting to discuss and resolve difficult and divisive issues is more exciting in the planning than in the execution. But I continue to believe it can be done.

Some background: Paul and Barnabas were doing a good job of evangelism in Antioch. Too good. There was a great influx of Gentiles into the rapidly growing community of faith. Some of the Jewish Christians in Judea were disturbed. They came to Antioch and began to teach the Gentile converts that unless they were circumcised and kept the law of Moses they could not be saved. In other words, before these Gentiles could become Christians, they first had to become Jews.

Paul and Barnabas disagreed and took on, both in private discussion and public debate, those they considered to be Judean troublemakers. They came to no resolution of the matter; the church at Antioch appointed Paul and Barnabas along with others to go and discuss the question with the mother church in Jerusalem. The result of that discussion is something almost unheard of in our day: the reaching of a genuine consensus. We are shown how to do this in what I used to call three easy steps; they are really not quite as easy as I first supposed. They remain, however, the three steps to good church conflict and reaching a consensus.

Step One: Information and Leadership

The story is told that during his first campaign against Eisenhower, Adlai Stevenson was approached by an enthusiastic woman supporter who said to him, "Governor, every thinking person will be voting for you." Stevenson replied, "Madam, that is not enough. I need a majority." Whether the majority of those in the Jerusalem church were thinking persons or not, those who spoke addressed them as though they were. One of the real temptations in discussion is to resort to what will win the point instead of that which will provide information and illumination on the subject. No name calling or appealing to emotions or reducing the matter to a few simple slogans in order to unleash a storm of hot passion. No appeal to either fear or anger.

Can you imagine how the issue might be managed today? I can just see the banners that those who came from Judea might have carried around in Antioch:

1. Which is it to be? Paul or Moses?
2. Since when are the Gentiles God's chosen people?
3. Who elected Paul and Barnabas?
4. Keep the faith: Don't let Paul destroy your church.
5. Paul is a liberal.

The problem with most meetings is that in presenting one's case, information often takes second place to emotion, passion, and the single goal of winning. Acts 15:12 tells us: *There was no further discussion, and everyone listened as Barnabas and Paul told about the miraculous signs and wonders God had done through them among the Gentiles.* From *The Speed of Trust* by Stephen Covey: "We've all heard the criticism 'he talks too much.' When was the last time you heard someone criticized for listening too much?"[8] It is time for a revolution. It is time for people to learn how to be silent and really listen! It is time for people to learn how to communicate real information. Paul and Barnabas gave full and complete information on what they had been doing in Antioch among the Gentiles. And these Jewish Christians in Jerusalem did the hard work of listening.

There is another interesting way to read Acts 15:12. When the Jerusalem Conference began, after the initial debate,

Peter spoke in favor of the Gentile mission. The text can mean that after he spoke there was a period of silence before Paul and Barnabas spoke. This indicates that those who were listening took time to absorb and mull over what Peter said. They were really listening!

The reason I title this first step "Information and Leadership" is because I think if it had not been for the leadership there would have been plenty of smoke and heat but very little clear vision and genuine light. The text seems to indicate that the first item on the agenda was general discussion and debate by everyone. Then after a reasonable but lengthy period of time, Peter stood as one of the real leaders and spoke his convictions. He must then have recognized Paul and Barnabas and asked them to give the details of their Gentile mission in Antioch. After they finished speaking, James, who appears to be the leader of the church, presented a summation and recommended a course of action.

Douglas Hall gives some questions we need to keep in mind:

1. Am I willing to learn from others without being an intellectual pushover?
2. Have I come to the point where I can understand why someone would take a different position from my own?
3. Do I reflect before I speak or am I more interested in making my next point?
4. Am I on a power trip – do I simply want to control what others are allowed to think?
5. When we discuss issues around the table, is it the most aggressive person who wins?
6. Are we really equipping people for the process of theological reflection or are we teaching them how to eviscerate fellow Christians?[9]

The discussion in Acts 15 had structure; competent, respected leadership provided order and movement. The meeting was not a free-for-all. Without respected and acknowledged leaders it would probably have been because this was a very hot issue with strong feelings all the way around.

Step Two: Full and Unhurried Discussion

Acts 15:7 states it plainly: *At the meeting, after a long discussion....* The question is "Why?" Because it was an important part of the process in determining what is frequently called "the will of God." They didn't short-circuit this process and neither should we. I would rather have people aggravated because there is too much discussion than because there is too little. The reason for the discussion is because those who had gone down to Antioch have genuine concern about the Gentile mission. They were not simply troublemakers; no one questioned their motives. None of those who came from Judea objected to preaching to Gentiles; they are concerned that those who come to the faith from a pagan background might fail to adopt the high moral standards of their new faith.

Madeleine L'Engle reports that her family was seated around the kitchen table one day when her husband and ten-year-old son got into a heated argument about baseball. The son said, "But Dad, you just don't understand." His father said, "It's not that I don't understand. I just don't agree with you." To which the son returned, "If you don't agree with me you don't understand."[10] Two quotes are in order:

> Everybody stands somewhere! Nobody has a God's-eye overview, and our own position needs to be open to question and discussion.[11]

> This side of the eschaton we only "know in part" (I Corinthians 13:12). Calvin said that no theologian is more than seventy percent correct. That may be generous.[12]

There will always be honest and sincere differences of opinion – even if all the facts are presented and people are able to understand. That is why there is a third step in this process.

Step Three: Compromise and Consensus and the Holy Spirit

One of my favorite truth-filled quotations is this one: "Life consists largely of solving problems, not in reaching some plateau where difficulties no longer exist."[13] I don't know how you solve most problems without compromise. Too many have the idea that the word compromise is unholy. Compromise is a necessity built into the fabric of life. What about these "wise" sayings that cancel out each other?

1. Look before you leap. He who hesitates is lost.
2. You can't teach an old dog new tricks. It's never too late to learn.
3. Out of sight, out of mind. Absence makes the heart grow fonder.
4. Two heads are better than one. If you want something done right, do it yourself.
5. Many hands make light work. Too many cooks spoil the broth.
6. Better safe than sorry. Nothing ventured, nothing gained.

The compromise that James suggests and is accepted by the others is really quite logical. Those who had gone to Antioch insisted that Gentile converts be circumcised and adhere strictly to the law of Moses. James offers a compromise: Gentile converts are called to live a high moral life and adhere to the Jewish dietary laws that would permit them to have table fellowship with Jewish believers. In this compromise, neither side got all it wanted. Gentile converts were not required to become Jews but they were asked to adhere to SOME Jewish regulations. These were the same requirements that had been set for strangers wanting to enjoy fellowship with conscientious Jews. This is what compromise is all about – give and take on both sides. What happened was that a way is found in which people really can be one in Christ Jesus and can have genuine *koinonia* (fellowship) with one another.

It is important to underscore the words that introduce the consensus and compromise: *It seemed good to the Holy Spirit and to us....* Another way to translate that: *It is the decision of the Holy Spirit, and our decision....* (Revised English Bible). What we are told is that the entire assembly "voted" on the matter and accepted the compromise offered by James with the feeling that God's Spirit (the Spirit of Jesus) had guided them in the process - in the process of discussion, debate, dialogue, offered compromise, and "vote taking." Here is a concrete demonstration of the reconciling power of the gospel.

Here is a powerful and provocative statement about the mission and witness of the church:

> If the church cannot demonstrate the reconciling power of Christ to the world, it will never be able to convince the world that it has any good news to offer....
>
> But if the world sees a lively discussion of differences taking place within a fellowship of love, where the discipline of trust carries across the abyss of disagreement, it make take a second look.
>
> The church is more than a political action group. It is a witness to the good news. It is in its very being a model of the Word made flesh. As Bonhoeffer noted, the church is nothing but a section of humanity in which Jesus Christ has taken form. The church is nothing but a section of pluralistic humanity – meat-eaters and

> abstainers, liberals and conservatives, Democrats and Republicans – a cross-section of humanity in which the reconciling reality of Christ has taken shape.[15]

A Final Question

We now find ourselves living in a culture that is a mixture of many faiths. Most never thought they would see a mosque in their neighborhood. Faiths other than Jewish and Christian abound. A major question for many is how to relate to those with a different faith. When I am asked if I believe that it is possible for persons of other faiths to "go to heaven," my response is the same as the one reportedly given by Billy Graham: "I have only one story to tell; that is the story and the witness I will continue to give. I leave the final judgment in the hands of God – where it belongs."

There are two dinner parties mentioned in the Gospels I would like to have attended. I would have been most interested in the conversation – which at most dinners of this sort would have been quite extended. The one is the dinner given by Matthew and the other is the dinner given by Zacchaeus. My reason for wanting to be in attendance is to listen to the conversation Jesus had with these groups of "sinners" – these groups of outsiders. All indications are that these people enjoyed being around Jesus. I don't believe they felt they were sitting under judgment and condemnation. Literally, they must have felt "graced." We are not given any details of the conversations or the result of those conversations in the lives of those who attended.

Biblical evidence points to Jesus and his disciples being welcomed by those the strict religious leaders of the day avoided and openly condemned. We are told that Zacchaeus was *trying to see who Jesus was* (New Revised Standard Version), *eager to see what Jesus looked like* (Revised English Bible). Wonder why Jesus held such an attraction for this despised member of his community? What was it about Jesus that caused so many who were put off by the religion of their day to be drawn to this man from Nazareth? Far too much evangelism is "preaching to the choir." It is designed to elicit a hearty "amen" from those who consider themselves to be safely in the fold. What do we have to say, how do we say it, to those who are outside our category of the redeemed?

Jesus must have listened as well as spoken to those at the dinner parties. The conversations reported in the Gospels give us an indication of listening on both sides. Conversation and dialogue begin with my willingness to listen to other people's stories and discover where they are. It has always seemed important to remember that Jesus did not have a prescribed "plan of salvation" he offered to the different people he encountered. Each of his conversations is "tailor-made" for individuals who have unique stories. Jesus does not say the same thing to Nicodemus that he says to the woman at the well. The man we call the "rich young ruler" does not hear the same thing Zacchaeus hears. The only single message I have ever found in any of the stories is, "Follow me." That parallels Jesus single command in what we call The Great Commission: "Make disciples." (That is the only verb in the sentence. B*aptizing* and *teaching* are both participles.)

How do we talk with people who don't believe we are really interested in anything they have to say? How to we share our story with people who feel we have no respect or appreciation for their story? How do we talk with people when we are really only interested in doing a monologue? Perhaps it is because we want to be able to say: "Well, I told them. Now it's up to them. My job is finished."

Some are going to be offended by this last bit; I'm willing to take the risk! When I was doing an interim in Athens, Georgia, in my book browsing, a title caught my attention. The title was *Lord, Save Us From Your Followers.* The author is Dan Merchant. Dan is known as the "bumper-sticker" man. Here is the opening paragraph from Chapter One:

> I think America has become a bumper-sticker culture – we're way too comfortable with one-

> way communication. We like to tell people what we think, but we don't like to listen and I fear we've lost the fine art of conversation – which explains why I was standing in Times Square on a late Tuesday night in December dressed like a human bumper sticker. Call this a creative attempt to resurrect dialogue and understanding – or as my wife affectionately put it, "I can't believe you're going to go out in public in that stupid suit just to have a conversation with a stranger." Yes, friends, desperate times demand desperate measures.[15]

Dan began all his conversations with, "Can I ask you five quick questions? They're easy." His five questions are:

1. How do you think the universe began?
2. Where do you think you'll go when you die?
3. Name something Jesus Christ is known for.
4. Name something Christians are known for.
5. Pick a bumper sticker. (The stickers represented differing points of view).

The people Dan meets and the conversations he records require you to keep your seat belt fastened! Nobody is ignored! You meet some of the most outrageous people you will probably ever meet anywhere else! (And isn't that a subject for discussion? Do we mix and mingle with those we believe are most in need of the Gospel? I usually don't!).

After I read the book, I immediately called a minister friend in another city and recommended the book to him. I gave him the name of the store where I purchased it; there was one in his city. A couple of days later he called to let me know that when he couldn't find the book, he asked a salesperson about it and was told, "We have removed that book from our shelves. I can't imagine why a minister would want to read it!" I returned to my store to get a copy for him and learned it had been removed; it had been banned. Big question: Why do so many outside the Christian community cry, "Lord, save us from your followers"? Why do so many outside the church have an attraction to Jesus but not to Christians?

Did this book make me uncomfortable? Of course it did! Anytime I have to look at myself and examine my motives and relationships and my witness for the cause of Christ, I get uncomfortable. Why? I might have to change! If we intend to reach our culture with the good news of the Gospel some changes may well be in order. We need to hear from the "other side." Banning a book that asks disturbing questions hardly seems the way to begin.

[1]Jason Bivins, *Religion of Fear* (Oxford, Oxford University Press, 2008), 232.
[2]Dan Merchant, *Lord, Save Us From Your Followers, 121.*
[3]Bob Sitz, *Not Trying Too Hard,* 111.
[4]Walter Brueggemann, *Mandate To Difference* (Louisville, John Knox, 2007), 73.
[5]Philip Gulley and James Mulholland, *If God Is Love* (New York, HarperCollins, 2004), 147.
[6]Ibid., 175.
[7]H. Jackson Brown, Jr., *Wit and Wisdom of the Peanut Butter Gang* (Nashville, Rutledge Hill Press, 1994).
[8]Stephen Covey, *The Speed of Trust* (New York, Free Press,2006), 209.
[9]Douglas John Hall, *The End of Christendom and the Future of Christianity* (Eugene, Oregon, Wipf & Stock, 2002), 192.
[10]Madeleine L'Engle, *A Circle of Quiet* (New York, HarperCollins, 1972), 195.
[11]David Ford, *The Shape of Living* (Grand Rapids, Baker Books, 1997), 30
[12]Douglas John Hall, *The End of Christendom and the Future of Christianity, 192.*
[13]Eugene Kennedy, *The Joy of Being Human* (Chicago, Thomas More Press, 1974), 151.
[14]William Willimon, *Acts, Interpretation Series* (Atlanta, John Knox Press, 1988), 130.
[15]W. Robert McClelland, *Worldly Spirituality* (CBP Press, 1990), 79-80.
[16]Dan Merchant, *Lord, Save Us From Your Followers,* 1.

The Time for Conversation and Dialogue
Points to Ponder

Argument is born of having the answer; conversation is born of having a question.

"Dialogue? If you have the truth what is there to dialogue about?"

When did we lose sight of the one thing Jesus said would mark us for the world as his followers?

The three steps to good church conflict and reaching a consensus: information and leadership, full and unhurried discussion, compromise and consensus and the Holy Spirit.

The problem with most meetings is that in presenting one's case, information often takes second place to emotion, passion, and the single goal of winning.

When is the last time you heard someone criticized for listening too much?

Have I come to the point where I can understand why someone would take a different position from my own?

When we discuss issues around the table, is it the most aggressive person who wins?

There will always be honest and sincere differences of opinion - even if all the facts are presented and people are able to understand.

I don't know how you solve most problems without compromise.

If the church cannot demonstrate the reconciling power of Christ to the world, it will never be able to convince the world that it has any good news to offer.

Conversation and dialogue begin with my willingness to listen to other people's stories and discover where they are.

Chapter 12: In Everything With Thanksgiving

MODERN OBSERVATIONS:

Gratitude, not understanding, is the secret to joy and equanimity.[1]

Instead of an agenda, I propose a *stance*, a stance of faith, joy, and celebration in the midst of postmodern mist.[2]

Archibald Hart: "Recapture the joy of little things."[3]

"Gratitude takes nothing for granted, is never unresponsive, is constantly awakening to new wonder and to praise of the goodness of God." Thomas Merton.

In college one of my jobs was opening the school cafeteria at 6:30 a.m. However, I didn't own an alarm clock. Another student left the boarding house at six, so I asked him to wake me. Recently, he reminded me that I awoke the same way every morning. I would shoot bolt upright in bed, stretch out my arms, and yell, "Good!" I may awake differently today, but I still say under my breath a loud *good* to the world. (Written at age 90).[4]

THE BIBLICAL TEXT: Philippians 4:4-7:

Rejoice in the Lord always; again I will say, Rejoice. Let your gentleness be known to everyone. The Lord is near. Do not worry about anything, but in everything by prayer and supplication with thanksgiving let your requests be make known God. And the peace of God, which surpasses all understanding, will guard your hearts and your minds in Christ Jesus.

Has Paul Lost His Mind?

In our text Paul seems to be making an unreasonable suggestion; when you discover the circumstances under which it is written it seems outright ludicrous. It sounds like a command: *Rejoice in the Lord always; again I will say, Rejoice.* Or it can be read: *Always be joyful...in the Lord; I repeat, be joyful.* This message, this command, comes from a man who is in prison with almost certain death awaiting him. Paul sends these words to the church at Philippi; it has become a part of Holy Scripture for every believer in every time and surely for our world at this time. Eugene Peterson in *The Message* gives this paraphrase:

> *Celebrate God all day, every day. I mean revel in him!...Don't fret or worry. Instead of worrying, pray. Let petitions and praise shape your worries into prayers, letting God know your concerns. Before you know it, a sense of God's wholeness, everything coming together for good, will come and settle you down. It's wonderful what happens when Christ displaces worry at the center of your life.*

All this sounds like a pretty impossible task. But in four brief packed verses Paul tells us how to do it – or at least how to make progress in that direction. That is all I have been able to do.

Many of the things in these verses sound strange to us but none more strange that these two sentences: *Let your gentleness be known to everyone. The Lord is near.* My emails recently carried some bits of wit and wisdom – with a large dose of humor:

1. I feel like I am diagonally parked in a parallel universe.
2. She's always late. Her ancestors arrived on the June Flower.
3. A day without sunshine is like, you know, night.
4. Hard work has a future payoff. Laziness

pays off now.

5. Since the fountain of youth has failed us, how about a fountain of smarts?

I will go a step further. How about a biblical fountain of smarts? A good alternate translation of Paul's *Let your gentleness be known to everyone* is: *Let your good sense be obvious to everybody* (New Jerusalem Bible). It has never been phrased better than this: "Modern man has been trying for nearly three hundred years to substitute faith in the future for faith in God, but the result is not making sense."[5] If we have the conviction that God is our hope and security for the present and for the future, then the others things in these verses do not sound so strange. Somewhere I found this: "Hope is the ability to hear the melody of the future. Faith is the courage to dance to it today."

Prayer Instead of Worry

Do not worry about anything is literally: *in nothing be anxious.* This cannot be the call to perfection. To never worry or never be anxious about anything is simply impossible.

> Lucy: Who's crabby?
> Linus: You're crabby. You're crabby in the morning, you're crabby at noon, You're crabby at night. (He begins walking away.)
> Lucy shouts: Can I help it if I was born with crabby genes?

Compare this with the plaintiff lament: "I'm a born worrier." Are we talking about worry genes?

One writer suggests that what Paul is after is that we get worry out of first place in our lives and get it in second place where it belongs. There is the place where it can be most readily handled.[5] That seems reasonable and a real possibility. Worries and anxieties will come but we don't have to dust off the best places in our mind and give them priority and prominence.

The kind of worry and anxiety indicted here has to do with being pulled apart or going to pieces.[6] A contemporary translation of what Paul is saying: "Don't let worry and anxiety pull you apart or cause you to go to pieces." The way he says to avoid this sounds so simple, but it is profound: *Worry about nothing, pray about everything.* It's the same advice stated differently in I Peter 5:7: *Cast all your anxiety – all your worry – on him, because he cares for you.*

The next item in Paul's recipe for good sense is the key ingredient.

The Attitude of Gratitude

In everything by prayer and supplication WITH THANKSGIVING let your requests be made know to God. Reading it from the New Jerusalem Bible: *tell God all your desires of every kind in prayer and petition shot through with gratitude.* All your desires of every kind. Don't hold back! Most praying is too reserved. We should begin with an honesty in prayer that matches that of the psalmists who were so honest that they sometimes charged God with being asleep on the job!

I love a twist on the old saying: "As you ramble through life, dear friend, whatever be your goal, Keep your eye upon the donut, and not upon the hole." The twist comes from a minister who used this saying in a workshop. He told the group that when we lose sight of what we have, we become consumed by what we don't have. Our vision then needs to be restored. We need to step back from the problem and gain our perspective so we can see the donut again. An angry woman yelled out in frustration, "You should see the size of the problem I have to deal with." The minister's response: "In such a case, the answer can only be, the bigger the hole, the bigger the donut." Paul is in a literal hole in prison. From there he writes what most consider his most inspirational letter.

In the Bible, there are more calls to praise and thanksgiving than there are calls to prayer. The only way you can really respond to these calls is to be aware of the giftedness and blessings in your life and acknowledge the source of all these gifts of grace. God's plan is to "gift" thanksgiving into us. The New Testament word for grace is also the word for gift. All is grace, all is gift. Life is gift, each day is a gift – a gift of grace. When you come at life like this everything takes on a different hue.

Some have labeled our culture "The Culture of Complaint." Certainly there is much to be unhappy about. The list of possible complaints has recently grown much larger. The people of Israel found much to complain about in the wilderness. Their "murmuring" punctuates the narrative. You wonder how they could so quickly forget their deliverance from Egypt and the mighty signs God gave them. It's the old "what have you done for me recently" syndrome.

In Maya Angelou's *Wouldn't Take Nothing for My Journey Now,* she has a chapter on complaining. When "whiners" came into her grandmother's store in Arkansas, after motioning Maya to move in close, she would bait them with, "How are you doing today?" As soon as the whiner left, this is what happened:

> And then she would say the same thing she had said at least a thousand times, it seemed to me. "Sister, did you hear what Brother So-and-So or Sister-Much-To-Do complained about? You heard that!" And I would nod and she would continue. "Sister, there are people who went to sleep all over the world last night, poor and rich and white and black, but they will never wake up again. Sister, those who expected to rise did not, their beds became their cooling boards and their blankets became their winding sheets. And those dead folks would give anything, anything at all for just five minutes of this weather or ten minutes of that plowing that person was grumbling about. So you watch yourself about complaining, Sister. What you're supposed to do

> when you don't like a thing is change it. If you can't change it, change the way you think about it. Don't complain.[7]

The attitude of gratitude is just that. It is a way of coming at life, it is a stance in life, it is a vision of life. Yogi Berra had a famous saying about baseball: "Ninety percent of this game is half-mental." That applies to gratitude - only more so! At ninety, Huston Smith has carried the attitude of gratitude into his 90th year.

> I could obsess about my ailments and be an old man in misery. Instead, I forget them and wonder how I came to be so fortunate and what I am even doing in an assisted-living home... I whisper under my breath, "God, you are so good to me" - thirty-five or forty times a day I say it. It seems I finally have a mantra.[8]

For the closing of his book *Tales of Wonder,* Huston Smith had three possibilities. He finally chose one he borrowed from the martyr John Chrysostom, who when he was dying exclaimed, "Praise, praise for everything. Thanks, thanks for it all." Huston writes: "I savor the words in my mind, roll them on my tongue, and repeat them as my own: "Thanks for everything! Praise for it all!"[9]

The Final Results

> Linus: I think you're afraid to be happy, Charlie Brown. Don't you think it would be good for you?
> Charlie Brown: I don't know....What are the side effects?

In everything with thanksgiving has a side effect: *And the peace of God, which surpasses all understanding, will guard your hearts and your minds in Christ Jesus.* This is the only place in the New Testament where you will find the phrase *the peace of God.* Elsewhere you will find the phrase *the God of peace.* The focus here is on the peace, the sense of security and well-being that comes not from any efforts on our part but as a blessing, as a gift from God.

It is such a gift from God that Paul uses a phrase to allow us to actually see it. The people to whom Paul writes live in Philippi, a city that is guarded by a Roman garrison. The Roman garrison is there to maintain peace and to guard against attack. Paul says: "As a result of your prayers, God's peace will stand like a guard to keep your hearts and minds safe from attacks of worries and anxieties." One writer has attempted to put the entire range of the thought of these verses like this:

> *It is my fondest wish that God's children be happy.*
> *I don't mean ecstatic or continually exuberant,*
> *I mean happy, full of joy, that deep-down contentment that persists even in the midst of trials and tribulations and difficult circumstances.*
> *As the very children of God, we really don't have a thing to worry about.*
> *Whatever our real needs, we know that God will fulfill them in His own time and in accordance with His will.*
> *We can well afford to celebrate,*
> *to live in thankfulness,*
> *and to allow the incomprehensible peace of God*
> *to mend the frayed edges of our troubled lives*
> *and make us serene and secure in our Christian faith.*[10]

[1]Anne Lamott, *Plan B* (New York, Riverhead Books, 2005), 295.

[2]Peter Leithart, *Solomon Among the Postmoderns* (Grand Rapids, Brazos Press, 2008), 14.

[3]Archibald Hart, *Thrilled To Death* (Nashville, Thomas Nelson, 2007), 151.

[4]Huston Smith, *Tales of Wonder*, xvii-xviii.

[5]*The Interpreter's Bible* (Nashville, Abingdon Press, 1955), XI, 110.

[6]*The Broadman Bible Commentary*, XI, 213.

[7]Maya Angelou, *Wouldn't Take Nothing For My Journey Now* (New York, Bantam Books, 1993), 85-87.

[8]Huston Smith, *Tales of Wonder*, 181.

[9]Ibid., 188.

[10]Leslie Bryandt, *Epistles Now* (St. Louis, Concordia Publishing House, 1976).

In Everything With Thanksgiving
Points to Ponder

How could Paul write his most inspirational letter from a prison cell?

How about a biblical fountain of smarts?

Modern man has been trying for nearly three hundred years to substitute faith in the future for faith in God.

When someone laments, "I'm a born worrier," are they talking about worry genes?

Worries and anxieties will come but we don't have to dust off the best places in our mind and give them priority and prominence.

Most praying is too reserved.

The bigger the hole, the bigger the donut.

In the Bible, there are more calls to praise and thanksgiving than there are calls to prayer.

If you can't change it, change the way you think about it.

Reflections on Part IV: Discovering Unique Opportunities

"If in the last few years you haven't discarded a major opinion or acquired a new one, check your pulse. You may be dead."[1] This may be the best test for keeping us informed as to how much aware we are of the newness that keeps coming into our lives. The question that follows the confession, "I don't believe we're in Kansas anymore," ought to be, "Where are we?" We need to keep taking a careful look at where we are and how we are.

Learning to live in difficult times requires that we become fully aware of the nature of the times in which we live. That we face the reality of what is. Many of Galileo's contemporaries continue to perplex me. After he discovered the moons of Jupiter, he invited those who taught with him at the University of Padua to look through his telescope for themselves. "Some of them refused outright, knowing that nothing less than their assiduously acquired Aristotelian understanding of the world was at stake. Some did look but incredibly reported that they saw no moon."[2]

I confess how difficult it is to look through new lenses and find it necessary to reorient your thinking about the order of things. My seminary education was not out of date – for its time. It did not, however, train me for the world in which I now live. Most of us never imagined such a world. It is still possible to join the "anti-Galileo association" and either refuse to look or to deny that you see anything you haven't always seen. For those who want to discover the unique opportunities of our present time, those are not options.

Whether we want to talk about "postmodern" or "post-denominational" or "post-church," it all means that old understandings of the world are no longer adequate. "Back to the future" is simply not going to happen. The fifties are not coming back. Sunday night services will not again become the norm. (When we discontinued the Sunday night services where I was serving as pastor, one member gave me a good verbal-thrashing.

When I protested that hardly anyone was attending, he protested, "Well, that may be so. But at least when people drove by the church they could see that the lights were on!") Now churches are finding alternative times (and even places) for worship, teaching, and ministry. The eleven o'clock hour on Sunday morning is no longer THE sacred hour. (Do you remember that this time was set when America was mostly rural and farmers needed to get their cows milked before they came to church?)

The questions we need to ask are not new but the answers may be. How can we be most effective in our mission and ministries? How can we be most effective in communicating the whole Gospel for the whole person? How can we be "user friendly" without being Gospel shallow? How can we best use the gifts of the people in our church to be the church God has called us to be in this place for this time?

Alan Alda in *Things I Overheard While Talking to Myself* relates the following experience:

> I sat next to a young woman on a plane once who bombarded me for five hours with how she had decided to be born again and so should I. I told her I was glad for her, but I hadn't used up being born the first time. Nothing stopped her. She was married to an acquaintance of mine, and I couldn't turn her off. I left the plane with an ache in my head the size of a grapefruit.[3]

I don't doubt for one moment the sincerity of the young woman. I seriously doubt the effectiveness of her witnessing approach. It doesn't sound as though she heard, or even asked for, any of Alda's story. Alda, who has been called by *Publisher's Weekly* "a Mr. Rogers for grownups," never heard anything that took into account where he was or how he was. The woman certainly never offered any good news; she seems only to have delivered a headache.

Walter Brueggemann has a sermon titled "A New Way of Being in the World." I quote at length because it is an excellent summary of Part IV:

> Jesus affirmed that it is possible to be in the world in a new way, to be present to people and problems around us with some newness and freshness....Too much of our repenting in this church (where he preached this sermon) has concerned trivialities that concerned neither God nor man.
>
> The usual way of being in the world is anxiety, of being pressed and harried and worried, and that in turn leads to a stance of defensiveness and fear and a determination to keep what we have.
>
> There are very few questions upon which it really matters if you are right or wrong. What matters much more, almost all the time, is to be able to enter into meaningful and serious dialogue with those who disagree with us. Being in the world in a new way means caring about communication, becoming sensitive, open and concerned enough both to speak and listen in healing ways.
>
> What matters is that I speak enough to share myself, that I listen enough to receive the other person in his fullness, that we commune enough that both of us can be changed.
>
> Being present in this way in the world is not a panacea that promises success, security or peace of mind....It can be the pause to decide again who we really want to be and where we would like to change, even it if means dying to something.[4]

In the Meantime . . .

[1] Gelett Burgess, quoted in Robert Wicks, *Everyday Simplicity* (Notre Dame, Sorin Books, 2003), 69.

[2]James Carse, *The Religious Case Against Belief* (New York, Penguin Press, 2008), 19.

[3]Alan Alda, *Things I Overheard While Talking To Myself* (New York, Random House, 2008) 8.

[4]Walter Brueggemann, *The Collected Sermons of Walter Brueggemann* (Louisville, Westminster John Knox, 2011), 341-345.

Conclusion: A Tough Faith For Tough Times

MODERN OBSERVATIONS:

Philip Yancey lists the three things his father-in-law believed at the end of his life: "Life is difficult. God is merciful. Heaven is sure."[1]

As one writer has put it, sometimes God calms the storm, but sometimes Gods lets the storm rage and calms the frightened child.[2]

From a sermon on I John 5:4: *This is the victory that has overcome the world, even our faith* (New International Version): "...the natural question for today in particular would be 'Have I that faith which overcomes the world?'"[3]

THE BIBLICAL TEXT: Mark 4:35-41:

On that day, when evening had come, he said to them, "Let us go across to the other side." And leaving the crowd behind, they took him with them in the boat, just as he was. Other boats were with him. A great windstorm arose, and the waves beat into the boat, so that the boat was already being swamped. But he was in the stern, asleep on the cushion; and they woke him and said to him, "Teacher, do you not care that we are perishing?" He woke up and rebuked the wind, and said to the sea, "Peace! Be still!" Then the wind ceased and there was a dead calm. He said to them, "Why are you afraid? Have you still no faith?" And they were filled with great awe and said to one another, "Who then is this, that even the wind and the sea obey him?"

Real Reasons To Be Afraid

These experienced fishermen, gripped by panic, woke Jesus because they felt this storm was about to do them in. They knew the Sea of Galilee, they knew the storms that came, and the danger from this one was quite real. The times in which we live are indeed stormy beyond anything most of us have ever experienced. At times, it does seem as though we are on the Costa Concordia and the Captain has abandoned ship! (This is the current major horror story on TV.)

Those who found themselves exiled in Babylon, Paul and Silas in an inner prison cell - they all needed a tough faith for truly tough times. Most any kind of faith will do in times of blessing, peace, and prosperity. Any old faith will do when the sun is shining. We have forgotten that faith in the Bible is not a sunshine faith. It is a tough faith for dark and stormy times. People of biblical faith could get up in the morning, know that their enemies were over the next hill, see the locusts swarming overhead, realize it hadn't rained for weeks and say, "*This is the day the Lord has made; let us rejoice and be glad in it.*" Most of us know little of this kind of faith. Jesus asks us the same question he asked the disciples that day, "Where is your faith? A faith adequate for tough times."

In a collection titled *Letters to Ministers,* Alfred Adler gives this one from Theresa, age 8: "Dear Minister, I know God loves me but I wish he would get me an 'A' on my report card so I could be sure." Faith cannot be dictated by the circumstances in which we find ourselves. It sounds like heresy but I assure you it is not: we don't judge whether or not God cares by what is happening to us and around us. In affirming that *nothing can separate us from the love of God that is in Christ Jesus our Lord,* Paul lists a whole lot of things that would appear to indicate God has abandoned us (Romans 8:35f). He has not simply fallen asleep, he has abandoned ship. Paul asks, "*Shall trouble or hardship or persecution or famine or nakedness or danger or sword*" separate us from the love of Christ? For most of us it certainly looks like it!

Paul and Silas are in jail for preaching the Gospel, for doing what they believe God is calling them to do. It is midnight and they are in chains...and they are singing psalms of praise and thanksgiving to God. They didn't doubt for one moment God's love; they didn't doubt for one moment that he cared for them, even though they were in prison.

At the end of World War II a group of underground fighters were discovered in a cellar in Prague. They had all been murdered by the Nazis who left in disorganized retreat. On the walls were messages written in various languages. One of the poems read:

> I believe in the sun when it is not shining.
> I believe in love, when I do not feel it.
> I believe in my Lord, Jesus, even when he is silent.

A quote I have never forgotten: "Never doubt in the dark what God told you in the light" (V. Raymond Edman).

A Tough Faith is Trust

Elsewhere I have written what I continue to believe: the opposite of faith is not doubt but fear. That is why Jesus asked, *"Why are you afraid? Where is your faith?"* Biblically, the word translated *believe* almost always means *trust.* John 14:1 in the King James is *Believe in God; believe also in me.* The better translation is: *Trust in God; trust also in me.* The basic meaning of this trust is to lean on, to rely upon. Biblical faith is a way of life, not a flashlight to turn on when it gets dark. Faith is a stance, an attitude.

In her *Prison Letters* Corrie ten Boom writes from a Nazi concentration camp:

> We did not know what was ahead of us, but I was certain of one thing – that Jesus would never leave us nor forsake us and that, for a child of God, no pit could be so deep that Jesus was not deeper still. During my months of solitary confinement, I often felt lonely and afraid. In such moments I recalled that last night with my

> elderly father, sharing Psalm 91 and praying. I could remember some of those verses, especially, *He shall cover thee with his feathers, and under his wings shalt thou trust: his truth shall be thy shield and buckler.* I would close my eyes and visualize that kind of protection. *He shall cover thee with his feathers,* and with that thought in mind, I would fall asleep. [4]

It is important to remember that we walk by faith and not by feelings. Feelings are often unreliable, especially during adverse conditions. I believe that feeling God is with us during desperate times is a special gift and blessing. We are assured he is with us, whether we feel his presence or not. When I prayed with patients in the hospital, I did not pray for God's awareness of them and their situation; my prayer was that we might be assured of the presence of God with us at that moment. The purpose of most prayer is not for us to get God's attention but for God to get our attention. I never believed when I visited that I was taking God to people. He was already there. Our task was to discover him together.

A Tough Faith is Expectant

Charlie Brown is in despair over his kite which is on the ground:

> Charlie Brown: I can't get that stupid kite in the air. I can't! I can't!
> Lucy: Oh, come on now, Charlie Brown. That's no way to talk. The whole trouble with you is you don't believe in yourself! You don't believe in your own abilities! You've got to say to yourself, 'I believe that I can fly this kite.' Now go ahead, say to yourself, 'I believe that I can fly this kite!'
> Charlie Brown: I believe that I can fly this kite.

Lucy: All right, now say it out loud...say it over and over...
Charlie Brown: I believe that I can fly this kite! I believe that I can fly this kite!
Lucy: You do? I'll bet you ten to one you're wrong!

Lucy knows Charlie Brown doesn't really expect to fly the kite. His words don't match the disability he carries within himself. Charlie Brown is not an expectant person, period. Genuine faith is expectant. The trouble with most of us is not that we expect too much but that we expect too little. An anonymous poem puts it in simple language:

Filled with a strange, new hope they came,
The blind, the leper, the sick, the lame.
Frail of body and spent of soul...
As many as touched Him were made whole.
On every tongue was the Healer's name,
Through all the country they spread His fame.
But doubt clung tight to his wooden crutch
Saying, "We must not expect too much."

Down through the ages a promise came,
Healing for sorrow and sin and shame,
Help for the helpless and sight for the blind,
Healing for the body and soul and mind.

The Christ we follow is still the same,
With blessings that all who will may claim.
But how often we miss Love's healing touch
By thinking, "We must not expect too much."

Expect life, love, joy, and fullness even in your wilderness experience, even in a world that isn't like Kansas anymore. Tough faith opens our eyes to new possibilities and opportunities in the most unlikely of times and the most unlikely of places.

Expect to be able to sing the Lord's song in a strange land. Expect to find something for which to be grateful during times of limitation. Most parents are reported to feel that their children will not have the same standard of living they have. Of course, that all depends on how you measure the "standard." It all depends on what criteria go into the mix. The standard of true living can go up even when times are at their worst. We make discoveries about relationships and small pleasures that escaped us during prosperous and seemingly carefree times.

One writer laments: "It is at the level of the imagination that contemporary life is weakest....The human capacity for reflection, intuition, and the development of the imagination is at an all-time low."[5] Tough faith is high in reflection, intuition, and imagination. That is why many reflect back on the toughest of times as some of the best of times. Not because they were difficult but because they formed the context for some significant achievements. Faith is always filled with imagination, with possibilities in the time and situation where it is located. It is possible to live a fulfilled life in Babylon. It is possible to live a fulfilled life while journeying through the wilderness. And it is possible even in a prison cell to find something of significance that can give life meaning.

Harold Kushner reports sitting with a teenage girl in his congregation who had just been diagnosed with a chronic illness that would severely limit her ability to do things that teenagers do – swimming, dancing, skiing. He said to her:

> Don't let this illness define who you are. Ninety-eight percent of you is just fine; there's just one little part of you that doesn't work right. Focus on the ninety-eight percent. You're still bright, attractive, caring, funny. Those are things your condition can't take away from you unless you let it. The choice is yours.[6]

That's the choice we all have to make during difficult

times. It is our choice that is the determining factor in just how much living we will do.

[1]Philip Yancey, *Reaching for the Invisible God* (Grand Rapids, Zondervan Publishing House, 2000), 92.

[2]Harold Kushner, *The Lord Is My Shepherd* (New York, Alfred A. Knopf, 2003), 8.

[3]John Keble, *Sermons for the Christian Year* (Grand Rapids, William B. Eerdmans, 2004), 126.

[4] Corrie ten Boom. *Prison Letters* (Grand Rapids, Fleming H. Revell, 1975), 12.

[5]Diamuid O'Murchu, *Quantum Theology,* 126.

[6]Harold Kushner, *The Lord Is My Shepherd, 159.*

Bibliography of Quoted Sources

Alda, Alan. *Things I Overheard While Talking To Myself.* New York: Random House, 2008.

Angelou, Maya. *Wouldn't Take Nothing For My Journey Now.* New York: Bantam Books, 1993.

Armstrong, Karen. *Twelve Steps to a Compassionate Life.* New York: Alfred A.Knopf, 2010.

Awbrey, David. *Finding Hope in the Age of Melancholy.* Boston: Little, Brown, 1999.

Barclay, William. *The Daily Study Bible: Corinthians.* Philadelphia: Westminster Press, 1956.

Barnett, Henlee. *A Pilgrimage of Faith.* Macon: Mercer University Press, 2004.

Bivins, Jason. *Religion of Fear.* Oxford: Oxford University Press, 2008.

Boom, Corrie ten Boom. *Prison Letters.* Grand Rapids: Fleming H. Revell, 1975.

Borg, Marcus. *Meeting Jesus Again for the First Time.* San Francisco: Harper SanFrancisco, 1995.

Boteach, Samuel. *Renewal.* New York: Basic Books, 2010.

Brauch, Manfred. *Abusing Scripture.* Downers Grove, Il. InterVarsity Press, 2009.

Broadman Bible Commentary. Nashville: Broadman Press, 1970.

Brown, Jr., H. Jackson. *Wit and Wisdom of the Peanut Butter Gang.* Nashville: Rutledge Hill Press, 1994.

Brueggemann, Walter. *An Unsettling God.* Minneapolis:

Fortress Press, 2009.

__________. *The Collected Sermons of Walter Brueggemann.* Louisville: Westminster John Knox, 2011.

__________. *Mandate to Difference.* Louisville: John Knox, 2007.

Bryandt, Leslie. *Epistles Now.* St. Louis: Concordia Publishing House, 1976.

Burke, Spencer. *Heretic's Guide to Eternity.* San Francisco: Jossey-Bass, 2006.

Callahan, David. *The Moral Center.* Orlando: Harcourt Books, 2006.

Capps, Donald. *A Time to Laugh.* New York: Continuum Publishing, 2005.

Carse, James. *The Religious Case Against Belief.* New York: Penguin Press, 2008.

Chittister, Joan. *Illuminated Life.* Maryknoll: Orbis Books, 2008.

__________. *New Designs.* Erie: Benevision, 2002.

Clapp, Rodney. *Tortured Wonders.* Grand Rapids: Brazos Press, 2006.

Couglin, Paul. *No More Christian Nice Guy.* Minneapolis: Bethany House, 2005.

Covey, Stephen. *The Speed of Trust.* New York: Free Press, 2006.

De Mello, Anthony. *One Minute Wisdom.* New York: Image Books, 1988.

Expositor's Bible Commentary. Grand Rapids: Zondervan, 1981.

Felber, Terry. *Am I Making Myself Clear?* Nashville: Thomas Nelson, 2002.

Ford, David. *The Shape of Living.* Grand Rapids: Baker Books, 1997.

Fosdick, Harry Emerson. *The Secret of Victorious Living.* New York: Harper & Brothers, 1934.

Foster, Richard. *Celebration of Discipline.* San Francisco: Harper & Row, 1978.

Gibbs, Nancy and Duffy, Michael. *The Preacher and the Presidents.* New York: Center Street, 2007.

Goldberg, Philip. *Roadsigns on the Spiritual Path.* Boulder: Sentient Publications, 2006.

Gordon, Arthur. *A Touch of Wonder.* New York: Revell, 1974.

Greeley, Andrew. *Sacraments of Love.* New York: Crossroad, 1994.

Gulley, Philip and Mulholland, James. *If God Is Love.* New York: HarperCollins, 2004.

Hall, Douglas John. The End of Christendom and the Future of Christianity. Eugene, Or.: Wipf & Stock, 2002.

Hall, Douglas John. *Thinking the Faith.* Minneapolis: Augsburg, 1989.

Hart, Archibald. *Thrilled to Death.* Nashville: Thomas Nelson, 2007.

Interpreter's Bible. Nashville: Abingdon Press, 1955.

Johnson, Paul. *Jesus.* New York: Viking, 2010.

Jones, Timothy. *Awake My Soul.* New York: Doubleday, 1999.

Jones, W. Paul. *Trumpet At Full Moon.* Louisville: Westminster/John Knox, 1992.

Kabat-Zinn, Jan. *Wherever You Go There You Are.* New York: Hyperion, 1994.

Kalas, J. Ellsworth. *Grace in a Tree Stump.* Louisville: Westminster John Knox, 2005.

Karon, Jan. *A Continual Feast.* New York: Penguin Group, 2005.

Keble, John. *Sermons for the Christian Year.* Grand Rapids: William B. Eerdmans, 2004.

Kelly, Matthew. *Perfectly Yourself.* New York: Ballantine Books, 2006.

__________. *The Rhythm of Life.* New York: Simon & Schuster, 2004.

Kelsey, Morton. *Christo-Psychology.* New York: Crossroad, 1984.

__________. *Reaching.* San Francisco: Harper & Row, 1989.

Kennedy, Eugene. *The Joy of Being Human.* Chicago: Thomas More Press, 1974.

Kidd, Sue Monk. *When the Heart Waits.* New York: HarperOne, 1990.

Kornfield, Jack and Feldman, Christina. *Soul Food.* San Francisco: HarperSanFrancisco, 1991.

Kushner, Harold. *The Lord Is My Shepherd.* New York: Alfred A. Knopf, 2003.

Lamott, Anne. *Plan B.* New York: Riverhead Books, 2005.

L'Engle, Madeleine. *A Circle of Quiet.* New York:

HarperCollins, 1972.

Leithart, Peter. *Solomon Among the Postmoderns.* Grand Rapids: Brazos Press, 2008.

Lesser, Elizabeth. *The New American Spirituality.* New York: Random House, 1999.

Macy, Howard. *Laughing Pilgrims.* Waynesboro, Ga.: Paternoster Press, 2006.

Manning, Brenning. *The Relentless Tenderness of Jesus.* Grand Rapids: Revell, 2008.

Mays, James L. *Interpretation: Psalms.* Louisville: John Knox, 1994.

McClelland, W. Robert. *Worldly Spirituality.* CBP Press, 1990.

Merchant, Dan. *Lord, Save Us From Your Followers.* Nashville: Thomas Nelson, 2008.

Monks of New Skete. *In the Spirit of Happiness.* Boston: Little, Brown, and Company, 1999.

Norris, Kathleen. *Acadia & Me.* New York: Riverhead Books, 2008.

Nouwen, Henri. *The Way of the Heart.* New York: Seabury Press, 1981.

Noyce, Gaylord. *Why Can't I Believe?* St. Louis: Chalice Press, 1999.

Oates, Wayne. *The Struggle To Be Free.* Philadelphia: Westminster Press, 1983.

O'Murcho, Diamund. *Quantum Theology.* New York: Crossroad Publishing, 2004.

Pagitt, Doug and Jones, Tony. *Emergent Manifesto of Hope.* Grand Rapids: Baker Books, 2007.

Pearson, Carlton. *The Gospel of Inclusion.* New York: Simon & Schuster, 2006.

Peck, Scott. *The Road Less Traveled.* New York: Simon and Schuster, 1978.

Pinchbeck, Daniel. *2012.* New York: Penguin Group, 2008.

Pinches, Charles. *A Gathering of Memories.* Grand Rapids: Brazos Press, 2006.

Powell, John. *The Secret of Staying in Love.* Niles, Il.: Argus Communications, 1974.

Powers, John. *And Grace Will Lead Me Home.* New York: McCracken Press, 1994.

Reece, Eric. *An American Gospel.* New York: Riverside Books, 2009.

Rohr, Richard. *Hope Against Darkness.* Cincinnati: St. Anthony Messenger Press, 2001.

__________. *The Naked Now.* New York: Crossroad Publishing, 2009.

Ruden, Sarah. *Paul Among the People.* New York: Pantheon Books, 2010.

Russell, A. J., ed. *God Calling.* New York: Dodd, Mead, & Co., 1945.

Samra, Cal. *The Joyful Christ.* San Francisco: Harper & Row, 1985.

Seamands, David. *Redeeming the Past.* Colorado Springs: Victor Press, 2002.

Shakespeare, William. *As You Like It.*

__________. *The Tragedy of Macbeth.*

Shortt, Rupert. *God's Advocates.* London: Darton, Longman, and Todd, 2005.

Sitz, Bob. *Not Trying Too Hard.* Washington: Alban Institute, 2001.

Smedes, Lewis. *A Pretty Good Person.* New York: Harper & Row, 1990.

Smith, Huston. *Tales of Wonder.* New York: HarperOne, 2009.

Sparks, Susan. *Laugh Your Way to Grace.* Woodstock: Skylight Paths, 2010.

Taylor, Barbara Brown. *Speaking of Sin.* Boston: Cowley Publications, 2000.

Thiel, John E. *God, Evil, and Innocent Suffering.* New York: Crossroad Publishing, 2002.

Veninga, Robert. *A Gift of Hope.* New York: Ballantine Books, 1985.

Weatherhead, Leslie. *The Will of God.* Nashville: Abingdon Press, 1944.

Weaver, Douglas. *From Our Christian Heritage.* Macon: Smyth & Helwys, 1997.

Wicks, Robert. *Everyday Simplicity.* Notre Dame: Sorin Books, 2003.

Willimon, William. *Acts, Interpretation Series.* Atlanta: John Knox Press, 1988.

Wright, N. T. *The Last Word.* San Francisco: HarperSanFrancisco, 2005.

Yancey, Philip. *Reaching for the Invisible God.* Grand Rapids: Zondervan Publishing House, 2000.

_________. *Soul Survivor.* New York: Doubleday,

2003.

Yrigoyen, Jr., Charles. *John Wesley.* Nashville: Abingdon Press, 1996.

About the Author

After many years of pastoral ministry, the author is now a Certified Church Consultant and an Intentional Interim Ministry Specialist (both through the Center for Congregational Health). He also conducts workshops on this and his two previous books: *From Fear to Faith: the Spiritual Journey from Anxiety to Trust* and *But If Not: Mastering the Art of Letting Go.* All three of these publications are available through Parson's Porch.

He and his wife live in Prospect, Kentucky. They have two grown sons who live in Atlanta.

His email address is rbooks5000@aol.com.

www.ingramcontent.com/pod-product-compliance
Lightning Source LLC
Chambersburg PA
CBHW060049100426
42742CB00014B/2753
* 9 7 8 1 9 3 6 9 1 2 4 5 2 *